Polikarpov Figh

in action Pt. 1

By Hans-Heiri Stapfer
Color by Don Greer
Illustrated by Joe Sewell

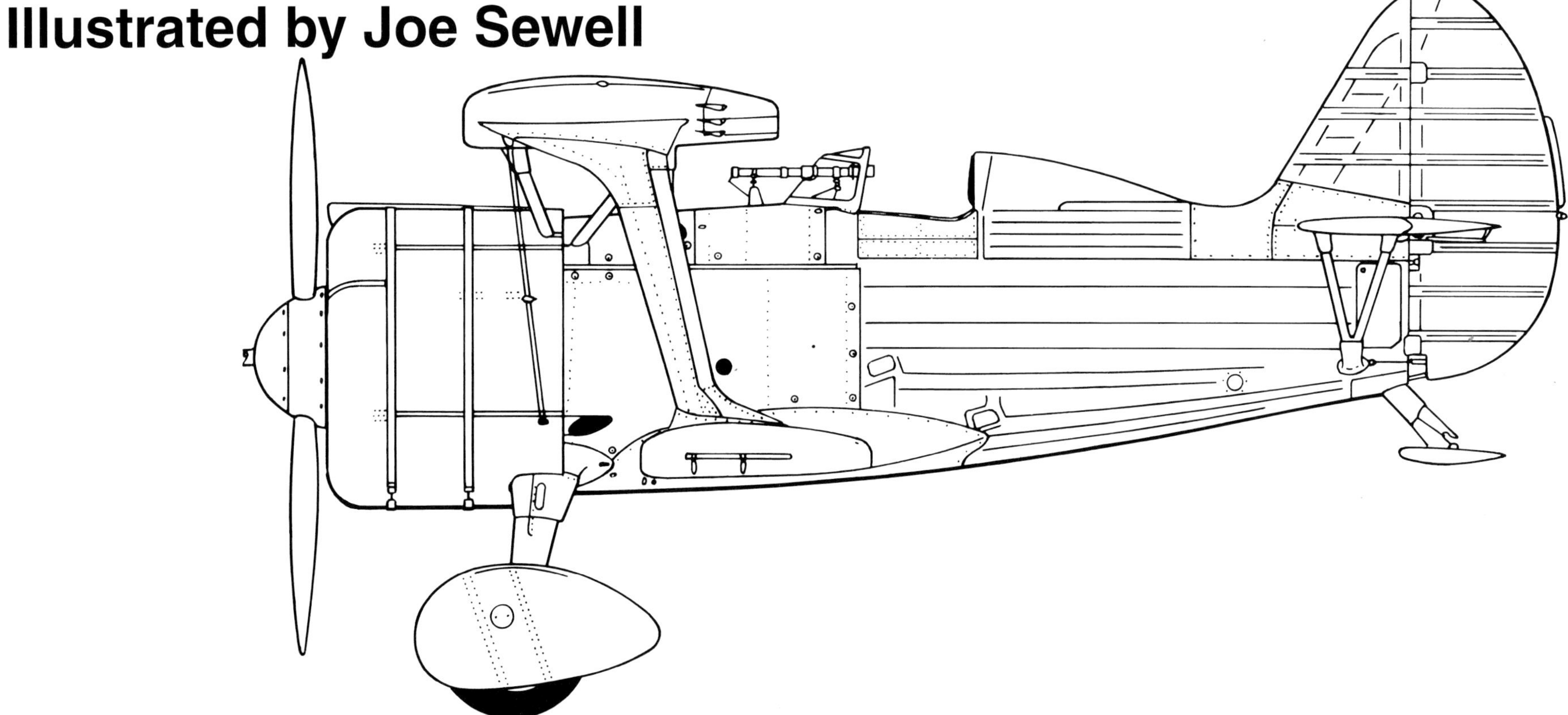

Aircraft Number 157
squadron/signal publications

Lieutenant L. G. Butelin climbs into position to attack a flight of Ju-88 bombers on 22 July 1941. Out of ammunition, he rammed one of the bombers, cutting off its tail. His I-153 was severely damaged in the engagement and crashed, killing Lieutenant Butelin.

Dedication

"Polikarpov Fighters in action", is the tenth "in action" book that I have compiled for squadron/signal publications and I think it is appropriate to dedicate this "in action" to the squadron/signal staff. I am always amazed how Nick Waters manages to translate my German/English manuscripts into Americanese. Don Greer takes my drawing references and turns them into great color paintings, and Perry Manley and Joe Sewell do the same with the line drawings. Last, but not least, I would like to take this opportunity to say a sincere "Thank You" to Mr. Jerry Campbell for giving me the opportunity to write for squadron/signal

Acknowledgements

Viktor Kulikow
Mariusz Zimny
Klaus Niska
Heinz J. Nowarra
Angelo Gentina
Dr. Volker Koos
Odon Horvath
Marc Bressan
Wolfgang Tamme
Attila Bonhardt
Harold Thiele
James V. Crow
Nicholas J. Waters III
San Diego Aerospace Museum
Robert Bock
Hannu Valtonen
Andrzej Morga1a
Yefim Gordon
Justo Miranda
E.C.P.A.
Martin Kyburz
Hans-Joachim Mau
George Punka
G.F. Petrov
Dave Hatherell
Andrew Zinchuck
Keski-Suomen - Ilmailumuseon
Robert Gretzyngier
A. A. Zirnov
Bundesarchive Koblenz
Museo del Aire - Madrid
Juan Arraez Cerda
Heinz Birkholz
Ray Wagner
Nigel A. Eastaway
Hadtorteneti Muzeum
Zdenek Hurt
Dusan Mikolas
Bundesarchiv Koblenz
Frieder Voigt
Henry Hoppe
Gunter Metzner
Thomas Heinicke
Renald Gravel
Christoph Stuker
Andras Nagy
Denes Bernard
Dan Antoniu
Martin Dotsky
Ivan Ivanow

ISBN 0-89747-343-4

If you have any photographs of aircraft, armor, soldiers, or ships of any nation, particularly wartime snapshots, why not share them with us and help make Squadron/Signal's books all the more interesting and complete in the future. Any photograph sent to us will be copied and the original returned. The donor will be fully credited for any photos used. Please send them to:

Squadron/Signal Publications, Inc.
1115 Crowley Drive
Carrollton, TX 75011-5010

Если у вас есть фотографии самолётов, вооружения, солдат или кораблей любой страны, особенно, снимки времён войны, поделитесь с нами и помогите сделать новые книги издательства Эскадрон/Сигнал ещё интереснее. Мы переснимем ваши фотографии и вернём оригиналы. Имена приславших снимки будут сопровождать все опубликованные фотографии. Пожалуйста, присылайте фотографии по адресу:

Squadron/Signal Publications, Inc.
1115 Crowley Drive
Carrollton, TX 75011-5010

軍用機、装甲車両、兵士、軍艦などの写真を所持しておられる方はいらっしゃいませんか？どの国のものでも結構です。作戦中に撮影されたものが特に良いのです。Squadron/Signal社の出版する刊行物において、このような写真は内容を一層充実し、興味深くすることができます。当方にお送り頂いた写真は、複写の後お返しいたします。出版物中に写真を使用した場合は、必ず提供者のお名前を明記させて頂きます。お写真は下記にご送付ください。

Squadron/Signal Publications, Inc.
1115 Crowley Drive
Carrollton, TX 75011-5010

When Germany invaded the Soviet Union on 22 June 1941, the Polikarpov fighter biplanes, which made up a significant part of the Red Air Force, were hopelessly outclassed by the Messerschmitt Bf-109 fighters of the Luftwaffe. Many were destroyed on the ground, such as these I-152s on a Ukrainian airfield, before they could engage the Luftwaffe.

Introduction

The nimble, little biplane fighters developed by Nikolai Nikolayevich Polikarpov were, without doubt, the most prominent and successful Soviet biplane fighter designs produced during the interwar years.

Polikarpov was born on 8 July 1892. He graduated from the Polytechnical Institute of Petrograd as a mechanic and aero engineer during early 1916, and remained in Russia after the Bolshevik Revolution of 7 November 1917, even declining an invitation from his former employer, Igor Sikorsky, to work in the United States. This loyalty was soon rewarded by the Communists and, in the early 1920s, he became the chief designer of State Aircraft Factory Number One.

During the 1930s, Polikarpov's fighter designs became the backbone of the Soviet Air Force. In the early Forties, Polikarpov, once called the "Fighter King," was surpassed by younger designers, such as Alexander Yakovlev, and lost much of his influence on new fighter designs. A considerable number of skilled Polikarpov OKB engineers and workers followed Artyom Mikoyan and Mikhail Gurevich when they erected their own MiG Design Bureau in December of 1939. His last fighter projects, such as the I-180, were not competitive, when compared with the fighters being designed by Yakovlev, MiG, or LaGG design bureaus. He was still respected by Stalin and, in 1940, he was awarded the "Hero of the Socialist Labor" medal, and in 1941 and 1943, he also won the State Prize. After 1943, Polikarpov worked with the Moscow Aviation Institute. Shortly after he died in Moscow of a heart attack on 30 July 1944, his design bureau was closed and the most of the remaining staff, as well the inventory, was transferred to the Lavochkin OKB. In memory of his efforts on behalf of the Soviet aviation, the biplane U-2 was renamed into Po-2.

Polikarpov's designs; however, were always rather controversial and their development was protracted. While Polikarpov's I-16 was the world's first mass produced monoplane fighter with retractable landing gear, his I-153 biplane fighter was still being produced at the same time as the I-16. It was a tragic that the technical advantage that the Soviet Union possessed during the mid-thirties with the I-16 was not developed any further for nearly half a decade, by which time the aircraft had been surpassed by other nations. When the war with Germany started, the I-16 was the most advanced monoplane available in quanitity and the I-153 biplane remained the backbone of the Soviet Fighter Aviation Regiments.

The first VT-11 prototype runs up its Bristol Jupiter VII air-cooled radial engine before its maiden flight from Khodinka, Moscow's central aeroport on 29 April 1930, with test pilot Benedict L. Bukholts at the controls. The VT inside the star emblem on the tail stood for (*Vnutrennaya Tyurma*/Internal Prison). (Ivan Ivanow)

Part of this was directly due to the Soviet dictator, Stalin. Stalin had ruthlessly pushed the industrialization of the Soviet Union and, as a result, extraordinary results were achieved in the heavy industrial sector, although the interests of the consumer were virtually ignored. Production figures for aircraft increased dramatically. During 1930, the country produced about 860 aircraft, two years later production was sufficient to give the Red Air Force a strength of 2,500 front-line combat aircraft. One of the ways this extraordinary increase in industrial production was achieved was by the use of forced labor.

During 1935, the development of the I-16 monoplane fighter came to a standstill and would remain stagnant for five years. The Soviet Union still produced the I-153 in large numbers during 1940, when the rest of Europe, the United States and Japan had accepted the demise of the biplane fighter. One of the problems was that combat experience in Spain, where Stalin had shipped hundreds of aircraft and other equipment to the Republican forces, led many Soviet scientists and engineers to believe that the biplane fighter was still viable. One fact that was ignored was that the I-16 could use its speed advantage to break off combat at will.

In France, the MS-405-01 monoplane fighter took for the air for the first time on 8 August 1935. Half a year later, in England, the Spitfire made its first flight on 5 March 1936. These new aircraft with their low-wing configuration, enclosed cockpit, flaps and variable-pitch propellers were ignored by Polikarpov and the Soviet Air Force and no effort was made to initiate development of modern monoplane fighters.

Even the appearance of the German Messerschmitt Bf-109 in Spanish skies, which represented a quantum leap in fighter technology, since it was 100 mph faster than the Soviet I-16 and biplane I-15, was nearly ignored. The Soviet Union, during the mid-thirties, had been one of the leading nations in fighter development, now it lagged behind European and American standards. Until late 1940, the Soviet Union still built the I-153 in large numbers as its standard front-line fighter. Compared with the latest German fighter, the Focke Wulf Fw-190, which flew for the first time on 1 June 1939, there were light-years of technology improvements between the German fighter and the vintage I-153.

This omission and the complete underestimation of the monoplane fighter concept as the future of fighter developments during the mid-thirties had devastating results some six years later, when the superior Messerschmitt Bf-109 dominated the skies over the Soviet Union and "Stalin's Falcons" had virtually nothing with which to challenge them. Another problem was leadership. The Stalinist purges had wiped out half of the Soviet officer corps, with perhaps 35,000 men being shot. When German troops invaded the Soviet Union, the Red Army lacked skilled, well experienced officers to lead the nations defense.

Totally outdated when the Wehrmacht launched Operation BARBAROSSA on 22 June 1941, the Polikarpov fighters were, numerically, the most important fighter types in the inventory of the Soviet Air Force. A total of 1,762 I-153s and I-16s were allocated to the Regiments of the Western Military District. The initial Luftwaffe air strike was aimed to create havoc at the forward Soviet air bases. At sunrise, a major Luftwaffe force hit sixty-six airfields which housed nearly three-quarters of the Soviet combat aircraft on the front.

The Soviet pilots bravely defended their home land against the superior Luftwaffe, but the price they had to pay with their obsolete Polikarpovs was very high. Even as late as 1943, there were a number of I-152 and I-153 biplanes still in active front-line service. Armed with

RS-82 unguided air-to-ground rockets or bombs of various sizes, they performed quite well against enemy ground troops in the fighter-bomber role.

VT-11 (I-5 Prototype)

During 1928, Stalin emerged as the political successor to Lenin, who had died on 21 January 1924. He ruthlessly pushed forward a program of industrialization and established a totalitarian state under the control of the Communist Party.

The Five Year Plan for experimental aircraft design, as prepared by ***Aviatrust*** (Soviet Aviation Industry) during 1927 and as accepted by Stalin on 22 June 1928, contained an assignment for Andrei N. Tupolev to develop a single seat fighter, the I-5. This fighter was to be powered either by the British Bristol Jupiter VII nine cylinder, air-cooled, radial engine, or the experimental M-36 air-cooled radial power plant. The I-5 was to be of mixed construction and the delivery deadline was September of 1929. At the same time, Polikarpov received orders to develop the I-6 fighter, to be made primarily of wood, with a delivery deadline of July or August 1930.

Tupolev's fighter project I-5 (factory designation ANT-12) proceeded very slowly due to his envolvement with development of all-metal bomber aircraft. As a result, Polikarpov took over the responsibility for development on the I-5, which was, in many ways, similar to the I-6.

The deadlines set for the new fighters were, in many ways, totally unrealistic. The Soviet Air Force was still dependent on foreign supplies, especially in the field of power plants. Moreover, the nation was still so industrially backward that workmen had to cut every length of supporting wire and shape very propeller blade by hand. Under these conditions, it was impossible to produce new fighter designs in the quantities demanded by the Five Year Plan.

When there was no significant progress on the new fighter designs, Stalin ordered the Political Police of the People's Commissariat for Internal Affairs (NKVD) to arrest Polikarpov, together with Dimitri P. Grigorovich and other aviation designers. These men became part of a twenty-member design team at Hangar 7 of State Aircraft Factory 39. This facility was, in fact, a well guarded prison camp. There may have been as many as 450 aircraft engineers and designers arrested by the NKVD, with about 300 surviving to work in police supervised design bureaus.

Both, Polikarpov and Grigorovich were, at that time, among the most prominent fighter designers within the Soviet Union. With the slow development of the new I-5 fighter, which Stalin so eagerly wanted, Polikarpov was charged with "infiltrating the aircraft industry as an enemy." Initially, Polikarpov and Grigorovich worked separately on different I-5 designs, but, when it became clear that the Grigorovich product would not be accepted, he and his staff assisted the Polikarpov team in order to deliver the prototype under the deadline. On 28 March 1930, the wooden mock-up of the new fighter was shown to a Military Commission, and, after some minor changes, work started on the prototype at State Aircraft Factory Number 39. Initially, the time needed to build the VT-11 prototype, which was to be powered by a single Bristol Jupiter VII nine cylinder, air-cooled radial engine, was estimated to be two months, but, despite their strange working conditions, the prototype was actually completed within thirty days.

The highly polished, unarmed VT-11 prototype was taken to Moscow's Central Airfield for its maiden flight. It carried on the tail the letters "VT" (***Vnutrennaya Tyurma***/Internal Prison), boldly inscribed inside a Red star. On 29 April 1930, test pilot Benedict L. Bukholz took off for the VT-11's maiden flight.

The second prototype of the VT-11 was painted overall Olive Drab. It differed from the first prototype in having a rounded fin, a covering over the shock absorbers on the main landing gear legs and a Bristol Jupiter VI engine. The White inscription on the fuselage reads *Klim Voroshilov*. The aircraft was named for Stalin's spokesman and chief of the Red Air Force, Marshal Kliment E. Voroshilov. (Viktor Kulikov)

The first VT-11 was soon followed by a second prototype, which made its first flight on 22 May 1930. This aircraft was named ***Klim Voroshilov*** in honor of Kliment E. Voroshilov, who became Commissar and chairman of the Soviet Air Force.

The second prototype VT-11 was painted overall Olive Drab and differed from the first prototype in having a rounded fin. In addition, the rubber shock-absorbers on the main landing gear were covered on the second prototype and a pitot tube was fitted to the starboard N-shaped interplane strut. The second prototype was powered by a Bristol Jupiter VI engine in place of the earlier Jupiter VII. Both, the first and second prototypes were similar in dimensions, but the empty weight went from 2,024 pounds (919 kg) to 2,090 pounds (948 kg) and the maximum take-off weight rose from 2,934 pounds (1,331 kg) to 2.998 pounds (1,360 kg) on the second prototype. Performance also differed between the two aircraft. The first prototype had a speed of 148 mph (238 km/h), slightly slower than the second prototype which had a speed of 161.5 mph (260 km/h), The first VT-11 had a better service ceiling (25,590 feet, 7,800 meters) than the second prototype (2,460 feet, 7,500 meters) and the range also differed between the two aircraft, 435 miles (700 km) for the first prototype and 404 miles (650 km) for the second. The test pilots all highly praised the VT-11 for its exceptional handling qualities.

With the VT-11, the design team had provided Stalin with the fighter he wanted, and he released them from prison. Not all engineers had the same luck as Polikarpov's team. Throughout the aviation industry, there were some 450 designers and engineers arrested between 1934 and 1941. Of these, about 150 died.

Development

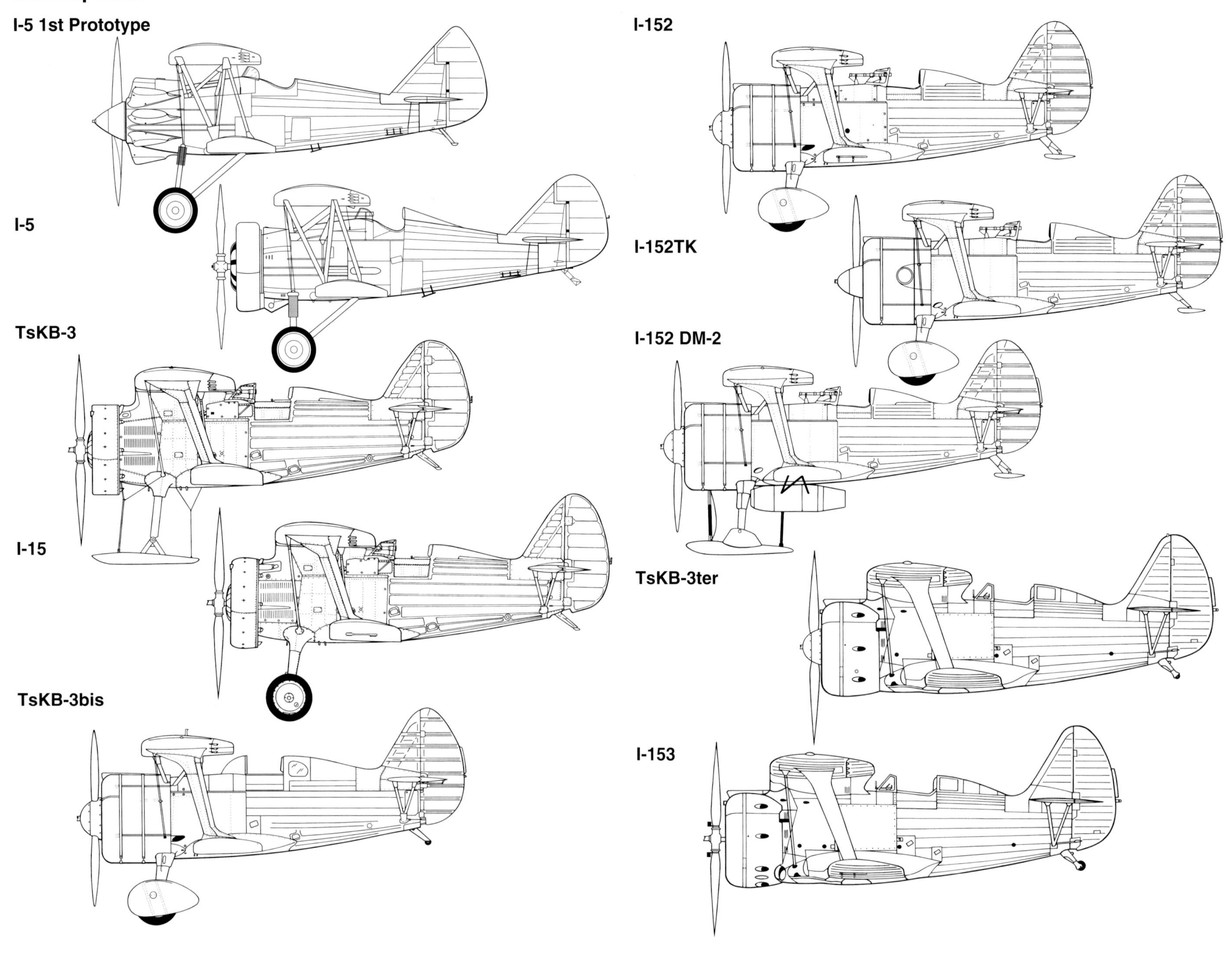

Pre-production I-5

In August and September of 1930, a small batch of seven pre-production VT-11 aircraft were built and allocated to the Scientific Test Institute of the Soviet Air Force (NII-VVS) for operational testing. These aircraft were nearly identical to the second prototype, apart from the addition of a small headrest fairing behind the cockpit, uncovered main wheels and a slightly redesigned tailskid. The ***Klim Voroshilov*** in turn was also progressively updated to near pre-production standards and also took part in the evaluation of the type. The aircraft was modified with the small headrest fairing and slightly different main wheels. In addition the exhaust stubs on the cylinder head coverings were also modified. The pitot tube on the starboard interwing N-strut, fitted during the factory testing, was deleted during the operational evaluation.

The evaluation revealed no serious complications to the general lay-out of the new fighter design and permission was given to begin production of the type under the Air Force designation I-5 (I =***Istrebitel***/Fighter). A special commission under the leadership of I. M. Kostkin was established to speed up the preparations for series production at State Aircraft Factory Number 21 at Nizhny-Novgorod on the Volga River. Preparations included the manufacture of molds and a full set of proper working drawings. This duty was assigned to engineer I.F. Florov, who was ordered to take over the preparation of the drawings. A number of undergraduates of the local technical college were drafted to assist him, since the prototype drawings did not exist. Details were made by hand, with dimensions listed on sketches which were hastily made. The only design documentation which had been made correctly were the static calculations, which Polikarpov had compiled into a huge book.

While preparations for series production of the I-5 continued, a third prototype was built. It differed from the first two in having a Soviet produced 450 hp M-15 nine cylinder high altitude rated radial engine. The Townend-ring cowling used on this prototype was identical to that which was later used on production aircraft. The interplane N-struts were considerable thicker than those on the first two prototypes and subsequent production aircraft. The third VT-11 also featured in a rear view mirror fitted on the starboard side of the upper wing.

The third prototype first flew on 1 July 1930, with I.U. Pavlov at the controls and was named ***Podarok XVI Partzjezdu*** (Gift to the 16th Party Congress). Tests and evaluation flights with the third prototype revealed that the M-15 power plant was not well suited as a production power plant for the I-5, but they also clearly showed that a Townend-ring cowling reduced drag and should be added to the production I-5.

The third prototype I-5, named *Gift to the 16th Party Congress*, made its first flight on 1 July 1930. It was powered by a Soviet manufactured M-15 power plant. The thick interplane N-struts would be modified on production I-5s. (Ivan Ivanow)

The second I-5 prototype was modified to near pre-production standards with a headrest fairing behind the cockpit and the pitot tube being deleted from the N-strut. (Victor Kulikov)

A pre-production I-5 undergoes static tests to determine the fighter's proper center of gravity (CG). (G.F. Petrov)

Development

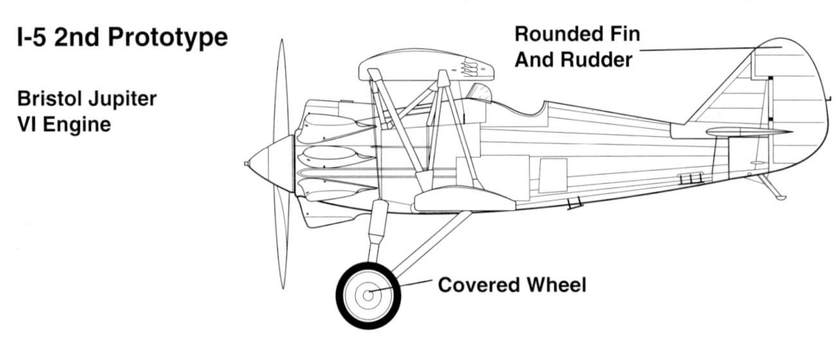

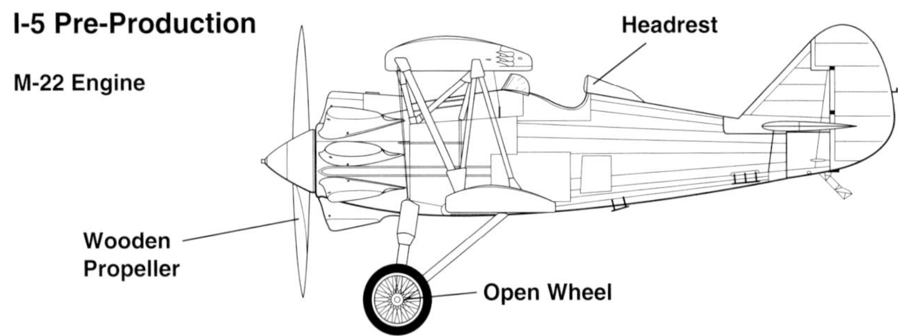

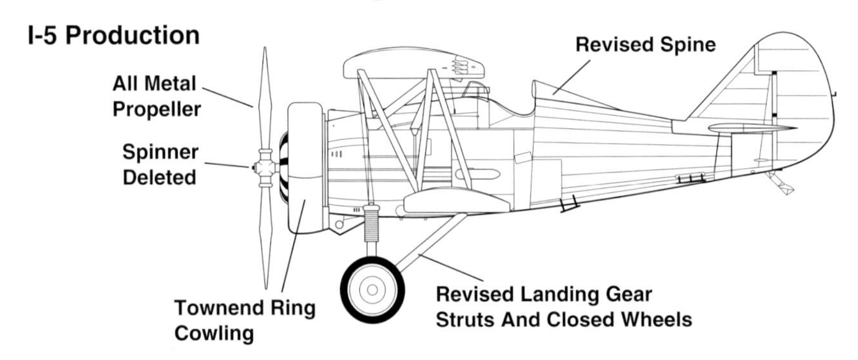

Polikarpov I-5

Due to the serious pre-production problems, it was not until late 1932 that full scale production was established at GAZ-21 (GAZ = ***Gosudarstvenny Aviatsionny Zavod***/State Aircraft Factory). The first I-5s off the production lines were assigned to combat units during February of 1933. From 1932 until the end of 1934, when the production of the I-5 was phased out, a total of 803 aircraft left the factory at Nizhny-Novgorod.

There were a number of differences between the pre-production I-5s and the production aircraft. The production aircraft had a NACA type ring cowling around the M-22 power plant,

A formation take off of civil registered I-5s. The aircraft on the left was SSSR-S2570, while the I-5 on the right was registered SSSR-S2590. Neither aircraft had the two synchronized PV-1 machine guns or OP-1 gunsight installed. (Yefim Gordon)

which was a Soviet copy of the British Bristol Jupiter, while the two VT-11 prototypes and the pre-production aircraft had a teardrop shaped cover for each cylinder head and its exhaust. Additionally, the spinner on early production aircraft was reduced in size. The 480 hp M-22 power plant was built in vast numbers until 1936. Although the M-22 was a copy of the British Jupiter VI engine, license negotiations and the supply of technical documentation and sample engines was done through the French license manufacturer, Gnome-Rhone.

While the VT-11 prototypes and pre-production I-5s were all unarmed, the armament specified for production I-5s comprised two synchronized 7.62MM PV-1 machine guns, with an ammunition supply of 600 rounds per gun and a rate of fire of 780 rounds per minute. In 1928, the PV-1 had became the standard aviation machine gun and was used on most Soviet fighters during the interwar years. Production aircraft were equipped with an OP-1 gunsight.

Compared with pre-production aircraft, the production I-5 had a considerably enlarged headrest fairing and an oil cooler was installed just behind the cowling. The shock-absorber covering on the main landing gear struts were reduced in size and the tires were slightly larger.

The I-5 fighter was of mixed construction. The fuselage framework was constructed of welded steel tubes covered with Duralumin (a light metal alloy) skin riveted to the frame. The nose section of the fuselage housed the engine bulkhead and engine mount which was made of

This rather worn I-5, White 6, was captured by the Germans during their rapid advance across Russia in June of 1941. This I-5 was a fighter-bomber version with two bomb racks mounted under the fuselage behind the landing gear. (Heinz J. Nowarra)

The cockpit side panel of this of I-5 has been removed revealing the synchronized PV-1 7.62mm machine gun. The PV-1 had an ammunition supply of 600 rounds and was the first aircraft machine gun mass produced in the Soviet Union. (Zdenek Hurt)

steel tube. The front section of the fuselage, as far back as the mid-cockpit position, was covered by easily detached Duralumin panels, while the remainder of the fuselage was fabric covered. The rear section of the fuselage, under the tailplane, had detachable aluminum panels permitting access to the tailskid suspension. The pilot's seat was made of corrugated Duralumin and there was provision for a seat type parachute. The I-5 had a fuel capacity of 54 gallons (205 liters) along with 10.5 gallons (40 liters) of castor oil lubricant.

A number of I-5s were outfitted with ski-landing gear in place of the standard wheel landing gear for operation from snow-covered airfields. These aircraft had a non-standard smaller propeller spinner and all-metal propeller. (Zdenek Hurt)

This I-5, Red 8, carried the tactical number on the fin with a thin White outline. The aircraft was equipped with an all-metal propeller and had balance weights on each wing tip. (Andrzej Morgala)

The upper wing was built in three sections. The upper wing center section was made of Duralumin and was attached to the fuselage by N-struts made of steel tubing. The outer wing sections were made of wood. The wing leading edges were plywood covered. The lower surface had plywood at the wing root, while the remainder of the wing had the plywood extending back to the front wing spar. The tail surfaces and the movable control surfaces, including the ailerons, were made of metal framing with fabric skinning.

The main wheels were sprung by sixteen rubber bungees 20mm thick. Initial production batches had a fixed tailskid to prevent ground looping. After several accidents the height of the tailskid was reduced and it was attached to the rudder post.

There were a number of detail changes during the production life of the I-5. Early aircraft all had a wooden 9.51 foot (2.9 meter) diameter propeller with metal covered leading edges and a small spinner. Later I-5s had an all-metal 8.85 foot (2.70 meter) diameter propeller without a spinner. This propeller could be adjusted in pitch on the ground before a mission.

Late production I-5 also had two tear drop shaped balance weights fitted on top of the upper wing near each wing tip.

Early production I-5s had a slightly longer main landing gear strut and a smaller shock absorber cover and as well open main wheels. Visually, these early I-5s could be distinguished by a slightly "forward" slant to the landing gear, caused by the larger rear strut. Late production batches had a shorter main landing gear strut and a larger shock absorber cover as

The forward fuselage, engine cover and main wheel covers of this I-5 are in Natural Metal, while the rear portion is Dark Olive Green. (G.F. Petrov)

A late production I-5 fitted with tear-drop shaped balance weights on top of the wing. The late I-5 had shorter main landing gear struts, an enlarged shock absorber cover and an all-metal propeller. (Victor Kulikov)

well as covered main wheels. Not all these changes were introduced at the same time on the production line at GAZ-21, and there were some hybrids that had late production type metal propellers but still had the early type landing gear.

Some late production examples also received, similar to the third VT-11 prototype, a single rear view mirror mounted on the starboard side of the upper wing.

A number of I-5s were fitted with a ski-type landing gear in place of the normal wheeled landing gear. A feature of these ski-equipped fighters was that they were equipped with the small spinner and all-metal propeller.

I-5s equipped the first Soviet Air Force aerobatic team under the leadership of V.A. Stepanchenok. Some surplus I-5s were even used with civil registrations, known codes were SSSR-S2570 and SSSR-S2590. These civil aerobatic I-5s had the PV-1 machine guns and OP-1 gunsight removed.

This I-5 was equipped with a radio. The antenna mast was fitted to the upper wing center section and the pitot tube was relocated to the top of the starboard interplane N-strut. Additionally, the aircraft was fitted with underwing bomb racks and large wheel pants. (Viktor Kulikov)

The I-5 continued to serve in small numbers during the Great Patriotic War (World War II). These Soviet Air Force pilots are in front of a late production I-5 during the Winter of 1941. (G.F. Petrov)

There were also trials conducted with radio equipment being installed on the I-5. Fighters equipped with radios had a large boom mounted on top of the wing to accommodate the radio antenna wires and further modifications were also made on the tailplane. These radio equipped I-5s were also fitted with large bubble shaped main wheel coverings and a large pitot tube on the port interplane N-strut.

The I-5 was withdrawn from front-line service during 1936, when the I-15s began to appear in numbers. Most of all remaining I-5s were then transferred to training units. Some aircraft; however, were modified as fighter-bombers, retrofitted with two bomb racks under the fuselage. These racks could accommodate two FAB general purpose bombs. When the Germans invaded the Soviet Union on 22 June 1941, there were still a number of I-5s on forward airfields in the Ukraine which were being used in the fighter-bomber role. A small number of I-5s were also transferred to Naval units. When the Great Patriotic War began, the 11th Fighter Regiment of the Black Sea Fleet, based at Jankoy Airfield near Sevastopol, was equipped with the I-5.

UTI-1 Trainer

This variant of the I-5 had the pilot's cockpit moved slightly forward and a second seat was added behind the front cockpit. This second cockpit was outfitted with a complete set of dual controls. Twenty aircraft were converted from I-5 fighter airframes at GAZ-21 at Nizhny-Novgorod during 1934, but they did not see active service.

I-5 *Zveno*

The term ***Zveno*** (Link) was used to identify a program, conducted under the supervision of military engineer Vladimir Sergeyevich Vakhmistrov during 1930 - 1940, aimed at creating composite aircraft. The concept was to combine a number of aircraft, closely linked together, in order to increase the range of fighter escorts for heavy bomber aircraft. All these trials

The first prototype TsKB-3 was powered by an American Wright-Cyclone SGR-1820 F-3 air-cooled radial engine. The aircraft had two small blister fairings fitted on the starboard lower wing, a feature found on the prototypes and pre-production models of the I-15. (Ivan Ivanow)

The overall Dark Olive Green TsKB-3 prototype did not carry national markings. The only markings carried were factory markings, which consisted of a Red star in a White circle on the fin and the numbers 39 and 3 in Black. (A.A. Zirnov)

give the pilot an improved field of view forward and upward.

The wing was built of wood, like in the I-5, with the "gull" portion of the wing being part of fuselage structure and made of a KhMA chrome-molybdenum-aluminum alloy framing. The fuselage was made of gas-welded KhMA tubing with a light secondary structure of rolled Duralumin, which resulted in a significant reduction of airframe weight, when compared to the I-5. Although fitted with a heavier engine, the first TsKB-3 prototype had an empty weight identical to a standard production I-5. The "gull" wing lowered wing loading, resulting in a highly significant increase in performance.

The first prototype of the new fighter emerged with the designation TsKB-3. It was powered by an American manufactured Wright SGR-1820 F-3 Cyclone engine driving an American manufactured Hamilton-Standard propeller. In the Soviet Union, the Wright engine was generally referred to as the RCF-3.

Armament for the TsKB-3 was comprised of four synchronized 7.62MM PV-1 machine guns with an OP-1 gunsight. There were also provisions for four bomb racks under the lower wing. In order not to delay the flight tests, the TsKB-3 prototype was outfitted with a ski-type landing gear and the first flight was made October of 1933 with Valerij P. Chkalov at the controls.

The factory tests of the TsKB-3 prototype only took twenty-six days, after which the new fighter was transferred to the Scientific Test Institute of the Soviet Air Force for State Acceptance Trials, which lasted a month. Both the factory and state acceptance trials revealed that the new fighter had excellent handling characteristic. During testing the prototype was able to make a full 360 degree circle in just over eight seconds, a dramatic improvement when compared with the 10.1 seconds it took an I-5 to complete the same maneuver. During the trials the TsKB-3 demonstrated a speed of 217 mph (350 km/h) at 9,842 feet (3,000 meters) and 201 mph (324 km/h) at sea level.

Later the overall Dark Green TsKB-3 prototype was modified with a stronger wheeled landing gear featuring an air/oil shock-absorber, and large streamlined wheel pants. The prototype carried no national markings, although it did carry a Red star on a White circle on the tail with the number 39 superimposed over the star. This was the markings for State Aircraft Factory 39. With the successful completion of all testing, the aircraft was cleared for production under the military designation I-15.

An overall Dark Olive Green pre-production I-15 at the Zhukovsky Test and Experimental Center (generally referred to as Ramenskoye in German intelligence reports). The two small fairings on starboard lower wing tip were only fitted to prototype and pre-production aircraft and were deleted on production I-15s. (Victor Kulikov)

Polikarpov I-15

Production of the I-15 started during 1934, with the pre-production and early production aircraft being equipped with imported Wright SGR-1820 F-3 Cyclone engines, supplied directly from the United States by the Wright Aeronautical Corporation of Patterson, New Jersey.

The reason for the use of imported engines was that it was found that license production of the RCF-3 would not be as easy as it was initially assumed. Work began on the project during 1932 at the newly established aero-engine factory, GAZ-19, at Perm. But, it was not until October of 1935, that the new engine, designated the M-25, was accepted and cleared for full production.

As a result, it was decided to power the early production I-15 with the M-22 engine equipped with a Stromberg NA-F7C carburetor, which was available in quantity, and driving a nine foot (2.80 meter) V-22 all-metal propeller. Trials showed that the 480 hp M-22 engine had little affect on the performance of the new fighter. At sea level, performance was even equal to the TsKB-3 prototype equipped with the more powerful 630 hp Wright-Cyclone. The M-22 powered fighters differed in having a slightly different engine cowling.

Between 1934 and 1936 there were 404 I-15s built with the M-22 power plant at GAZ-21. From late 1936 onward, the M-25 power plant became available for the I-15 and production shifted to this engine. There was a considerable improvement in performance with the new engine.

The M-22 powered I-15 had a top speed of 215.6 mph (347 km/h), while the M-25 equipped fighter had a top speed of 228 mph (367 km/h). The service ceiling was raised from 30,183 feet (9,200 meters) to 32,152 feet (9,800 meters) and the maximum range went from 298 miles (480 km) to 317 miles (510 km).

Ground crewmen help the pilot of this pre-production I-15, Red 3, prepare for another mission. The tactical number had a thin White outline and the national marking was only carried on the fuselage. This is a early style of Soviet star with a small Black circle within the Red star. (G.F. Petrov)

M-25 equipped aircraft had a V-25 propeller, which was a direct copy of the American

Development

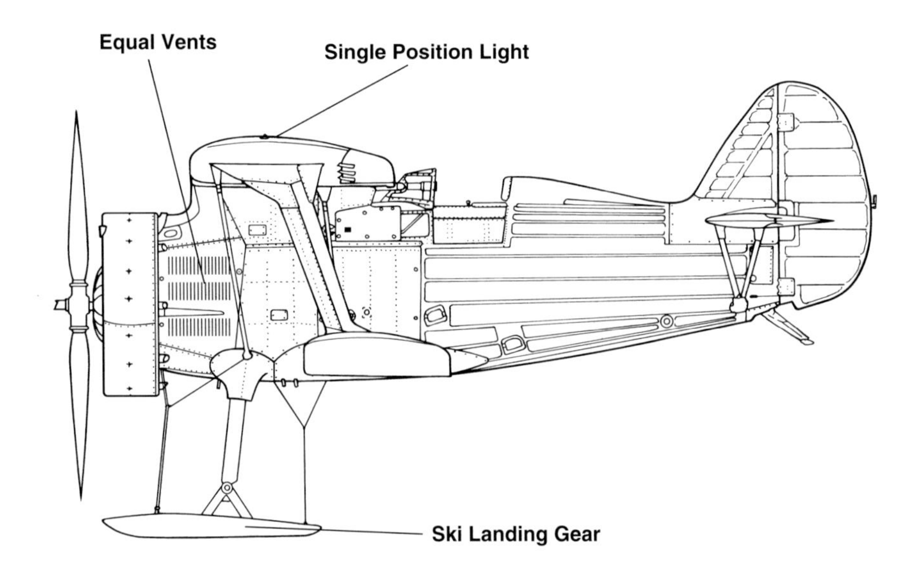

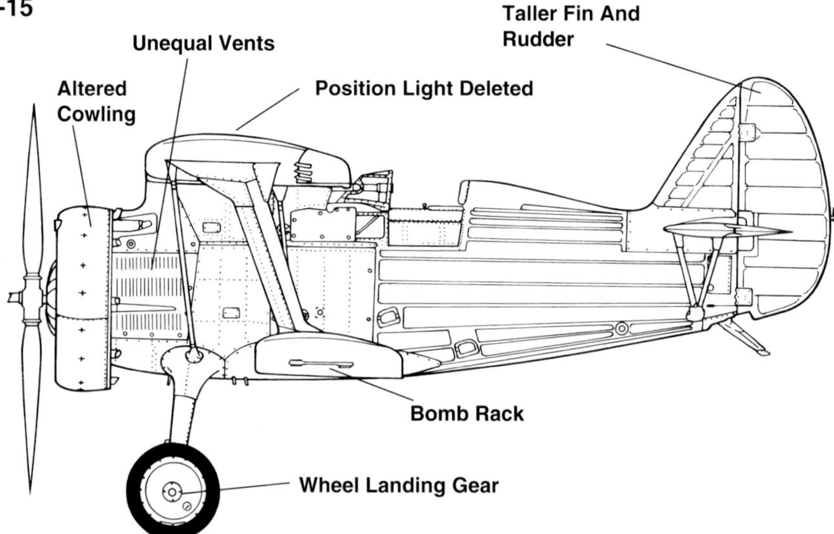

I. U. Pavlov poses beside his overall Silver I-15. The aircraft carried a Red flag on the fuselage side with the slogon, *Za VKP (6)* (For the Communist Party). The aircraft was used for demonstration flights. (Robert Bock)

Hamilton-Standard propeller. Some late production batches received the 538 hp M-25A power plant, equipped with a K-25-4D carburetor. These aircraft could be distinguished by an additional air intake on port side of the nose. Some M-25 powered I-15s were also equipped with the Vish-6 propeller (another Hamilton-Standard copy). Before production of the I-15 was phased out during 1937, a total of 270 M-25 powered I-15s were built. During the mid-thirties, the I-15 became the most important fighter in the Soviet inventory.

The production I-15 differed from the TsKB-3 prototype and pre-production aircraft. The TsKB-3 had three equal rows of equal sized vents behind the engine cowling, while production I-15s had three rows of different size vents. The TsKB-3 had a two piece pitot tube fitted

This Soviet Air Force I-15 nosed over after a hard landing. This fighter was unusual in that it carried no national markings or tactical numbers on the fuselage. (G.F. Fetrov)

PV-1 Machine Gun Development

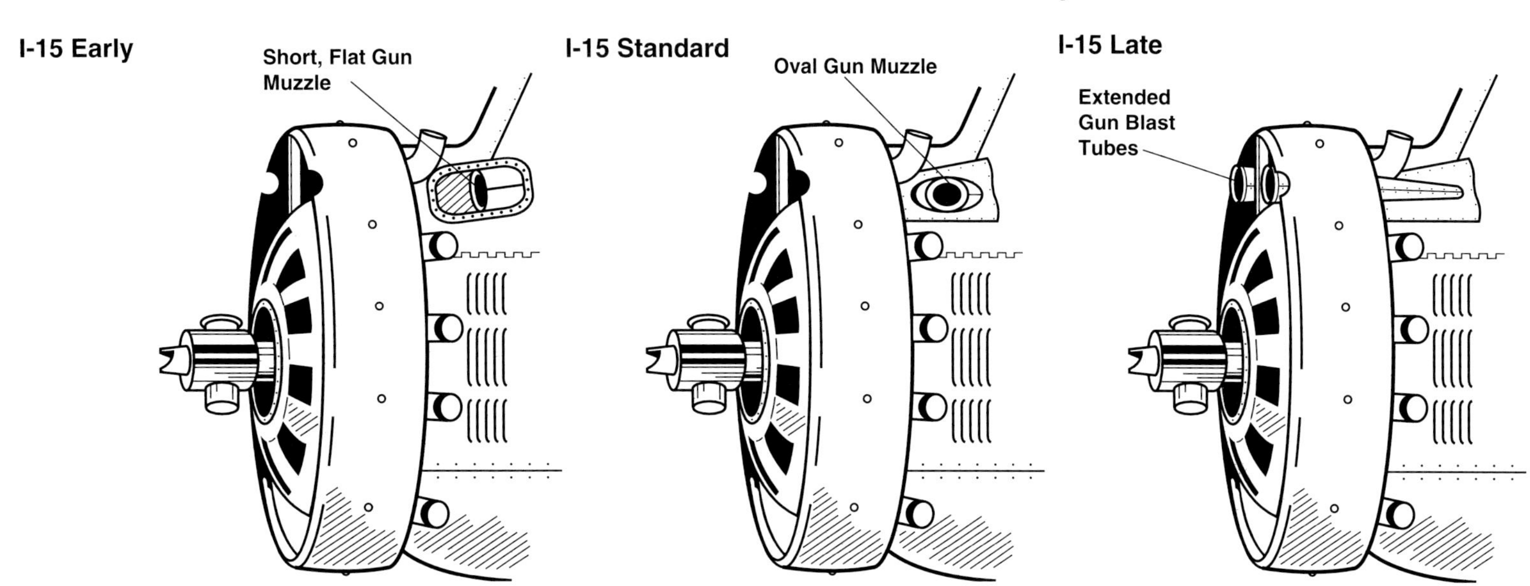

to the starboard interplane strut, while pre-production and all production I-15s had a single piece pitot tube mounted on a triangle shaped plate in the middle of the interplane strut. Both, TsKB-3 prototype and the pre-production I-15 had two blister fairings on the trailing edge of the starboard lower wing, which were deleted on production I-15s. Many production I-15s had the two under wing bomb removed. The prototype also had a tie-down ring under each wing, which was also deleted on the production I-15.

The most significant difference between the TsKB-3 prototype and production I-15s was the introduction of a taller, less pointed fin and rudder on all pre-production and production I-15s.

There were three different versions of the PV-1 gun muzzles. Early production I-15 had a flat type muzzle. While the later I-15s had slanting gun muzzles and very late production I-15s differed in having larger gun barrels.

Some pre-production and production I-15s were equipped with a rear view mirror mounted on the starboard side of the upper gull wing. Early production I-15s lacked position lights, but most later production aircraft had position lights on the rudder and upper wing.

The landing gear strut cylinders were originally round rods, but from the Autumn of 1934 on, they were made of rolled sheet metal with welded seams, and from early 1935, thick walled metal tubing was used. Similar to the prototype and the pre-production aircraft, some production I-15s were also equipped with streamlined wheel pants.

Some I-15s were equipped with RSI-3 radio equipment, with the antenna mast being mounted on the upper surface of the starboard wing.

The cockpit doors on the I-15 differed on each side of the aircraft. The door on the port side consisted of two pieces, while the starboard door was a single piece.

Despite the advantage the I-15 held over other fighters, its gull wing was not well liked by all. The airframe of the I-15 was of very light construction in order to save weight, but this weight saving meant that the aircraft was not as rugged as earlier fighters. As a result, a number of accidents occurred during normal air force operations. One problem was the failure of fabric on the wing surfaces. Landing gear failures were common due to hard landings on unprepared airstrips, and in some cases this would lead to failure of the engine bearers or fuselage structure. An improvement program aimed at eliminating the weak points of the I-15 progressed very slowly due to the excessive bureaucracy within the Soviet Air Force. Many front-line pilots also felt very uncomfortable with the gull wing and voiced a preference for the traditional straight center wing section.

Another defect that showed up when the aircraft was in use was the failure of the inner rubber covering of the fuel tank. This covering, probably of mediocre quality, deteriorated and fragments of the covering fowling the engine and sometimes causing it to fail due to fuel starvation.

Production I-15s were equipped with four PV-1 machine guns with 500 rounds per gun and had provision for either two 110 pound (50 kg), four 55 pound (25 kg) or eight 22 pound (10 kg) bomb on under wing bomb racks for close air support duties. Bomb types included the AO-10, AO-20M or FAB-50M bombs. In addition, six RS-82 unguided rockets could be mounted on Type RO under wing rocket rails.

When Germany attacked the Soviet Union on 22 June 1941, most I-15s had been relegated to training and liaison duties, however, the 3rd Fighter Regiment of the Black Sea Fleet based at Sevastopol was still equipped with the I-15 as a first-line fighter.

This I-15, White 016, was one of the first *Chatos* delivered to Spain. The first thirteen fighters arrived on board of the Soviet freighter BOLSHEVIK at Cartagena on 13 October 1936. (Museo del Aire)

Combat in Spain

Spain had become a Republic during 1931, and for the next two years the elected government pushed forward reforms intended to bring the country into the modern world. During 1936, the Spanish political left was dominated by the two general trade unions, the CNT, influenced by the anarchism of Bakunin, and the UGT, Marxist, but not Bolshevik. For the elections of February 1936, the Left came together, at the communists' suggestion, to form a

Teniente (Lieutenant) Romulo Negrin, son of the President of the Second Spanish Republic, poses along side his Soviet supplied I-15 (CC-011). Soviet-built I-15s received the code letters CC while all Spanish-manufactured *Chatos* carried the code CA on the fuselage. (Museo del Aire)

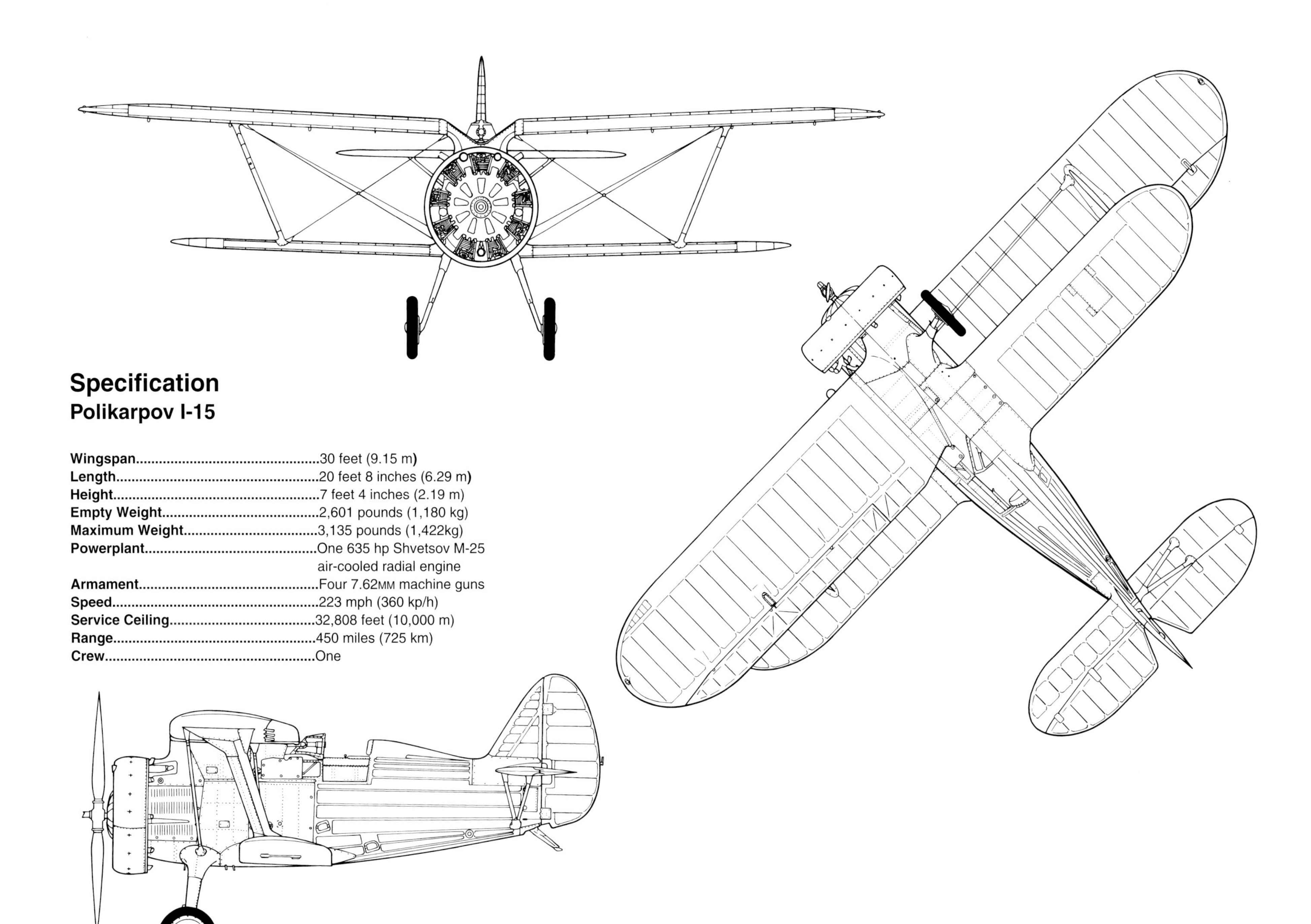

Specification
Polikarpov I-15

Wingspan	30 feet (9.15 m)
Length	20 feet 8 inches (6.29 m)
Height	7 feet 4 inches (2.19 m)
Empty Weight	2,601 pounds (1,180 kg)
Maximum Weight	3,135 pounds (1,422kg)
Powerplant	One 635 hp Shvetsov M-25 air-cooled radial engine
Armament	Four 7.62MM machine guns
Speed	223 mph (360 kp/h)
Service Ceiling	32,808 feet (10,000 m)
Range	450 miles (725 km)
Crew	One

A Spanish-built I-15 *Chato* of the 2nd *Escuadrilla* (2nd Squadron) warms up its engine on the grass at *La Aparecida* (Cartagena) during March of 1939. A short time later, the Spanish Civil War ended and many I-15s were taken over by the Nationalists. (Juan Arraez Cerda)

Frank G. Tinker, was one of the American pilots assigned to the *Lacalle* Squadron based at Azuqueca Aerodrome during April of 1937. Tinker was an ace with five kills and was the first American to shoot down a Bf-109. (Juan Arraez Cerda)

Harold E. Dahl, along side his *Chato* (CC-54) was one of several American volunteers who flew the I-15 fighter in combat over Spain. After scoring five kills he was shot down during 1937 and became a prisoneer for the rest of the war. In 1940 he was repatriated to the United States. (Juan Arraez Cerda)

Popular Front. The outcome of the election gave them 278 seats, with the communists holding seventeen.

On 18 July 1936, Nationalist factions under Generalisimo Francisco Franco rebelled against the democratic government of the Second Spanish Republic and, at the end of August, the Soviet Union elected to intervene actively in support of the Republicans. The reaction of the Soviet Union was dictated more by its fear of the growing Nazi movement and their Anti-Comintern Pact with Italy, then by the opportunity to promote the formation of a communist Spain.

In August of 1936, the Soviet Union established diplomatic relations with Spain and sent an ambassador with a formidable staff. This included General Jan K. Berzin, who had just left his post as head of the GRU (Soviet Military Intelligence). He played a major part in the defense of Madrid. Vladimir A. Antonov-Ovseenko, a leader of the October 1917 Revolution, was assigned as the Soviet Consul-General in Barcelona. Like so many other Soviet military

Scramble! A pilot of the 3rd Escuadrilla climbs into his Spanish built I-15 (CA-151) during the battle of Jarama. This *Chato* (CA-151) was built on 31 July 1938, and was the first I-15 built of the fourth production batch. (Museo del Aire)

advisors in Spain, both were later recalled to Moscow and subsequently executed.

Commander in Chief of the Soviet air component in Spain was Colonel Yakob Shmushkievich, alias General Douglas. Due to experience gained in Spain, he went on to assume command of the Soviet Air Force in September of 1939. After the ill-fated Winter War against Finland, he was removed from his post and subsequently executed in October of 1941.

Stalin committed himself to the supply of a variety of weapons, including the latest Soviet combat aircraft types, together with the personnel necessary to operate and maintain them. No fewer than a dozen vessels, allegedly bound for Mexico, sailed from Odessa and passed through the Bosphorus during the first three weeks of October carrying arms for Spain. Part of this shipment was a group of 141 Soviet pilots and nearly 2,000 technicians and mechanics.

On 13 October 1936, the first thirteen crated I-15s, which sailed aboard the Soviet vessel BOLSHEVIK, were unloaded in the port of Cartagena. Three days later twelve additional I-15 arrived at the same harbor. The Soviet Union, whose aviation industry was, to many western European observers, an enigma, had supplied its latest biplane fighter to the ***Fuerza Aereas Republicanas*** (FARE). Between Autumn of 1936 and July of 1937 a total of 186 I-15s were supplied at an unit price of $ 35,000 (USD).

While the first twenty-five I-15s delivered in October of 1936, had the M-22 power plant, the next batch of thirty-one aircraft arriving at Cartagena on 14 February 1937, were equipped with the M-25 engine. This indicates that the Soviet Union had shipped its latest variant to the ***Fuerza Aereas Republicanas*** as soon it became available.

The Republicans soon named the I-15 ***Chato*** (Snub-Nose), while Franco's Nationalists generally called the Soviet fighter "the Curtiss" because of its close resemblance to fighter designs of the Curtiss company, such as the Hawk II. Due to the fact that the Soviets had previously not released information on its fighter designs, it was generally assumed outside Russia, that the I-15 was a Soviet copy of an American and not a original Soviet design.

There were about six hundred Spanish airmen trained at Kirovabad in the Caucasus and at Kharkov in the Ukraine. But Soviet and Spanish pilots were not the only ones fighting with the ***Chato***. The ***Escuadrilla Lacalle***, named after Captain Andres Garcia Lacalle, also had a number of American pilots, who flew the Soviet I-15. Other foreign pilots fighting with the I-15 included the two Frenchmen, Jean Dary and William Labussiere, as well the Belgian, Andre Autrique. Similar to the ground forces, the ***Brigadas Internacionales***, which were formed with men from a number of European nations, the passports of these foreign soldiers were retained by the Spanish Republicans when they went to war. These International Brigades were all controlled and recruited by the Communist Party.

The American pilots flying the ***Chato*** in combat were not fully aware of the true origins of the I-15, and many believed that the Polikarpov fighter was a copy of current American biplane fighters such as the Boeing F4B-4. The international press took very little notice of the initial success of the nimble ***Chato*** when it first appeared during the battle for Madrid.

A number of American pilots became very successful with the I-15 during the Spanish civil war. Frank G. Tinker shot down three Heinkel He-51s, three Fiat CR.32s and two Messerschmitt Bf-109s, becoming the first American pilot to shoot down a Bf-109. Albert Baumler (who later went on to fly with the 23rd Fighter Group, USAAF, raising his total score to thirteen) succeeded in downing three Heinkel He-51s and two Fiat CR.32s, while James Peck had two Heinkel He-51s and three Fiat CR.32s to his credit. Orrin B. Bell downed seven Heinkels on the Cordoba-Granada front. Harold Dahl downed five Nationalist aircraft, including a Fiat CR.32 and a Heinkel He-51, while Ben Leider was credited with two Heinkels, before he was killed in action over Jarama on 18 February 1937. During the battle of Jarama, James Allison downed a Heinkel, the only kill claimed by this pilot. One Heinkel He-111 bomber was shot down over Madrid by Stephen Daduk.

The ***Chato*** came as a surprise for the Nationalists and it saw considerable combat during the

This Spanish-built I-15 (CA-063) was assigned to 2nd Escuadrilla (Squadron), Grupo No 26 at La Aparecida airfield during February of 1939. (Juan Arraez Cerda)

Battle of Madrid. On 4 November 1936, the I-15 claimed its first kill over Spain, when a Junkers Ju-52 bomber was shot down near Humanes. On 30 November, six I-15s of the Basque Squadron shot down two Heinkel He-51s over Vitoria. During the first air battles over Madrid the ***Chato*** proved to be superior in all respects to the German Heinkel He-51. But the losses were not one side; during November, the first month of operations in Spain at least fourteen I-15s were destroyed in battles over Madrid and the Aragon front; nine were shot down, three suffered accidents and two were captured. By the end of the year there were less than thirty I-15s operational in the ***Fuerza Aereas Republicanas***.

On 4 January 1937, two I-15 were lost in combat over Bilboa and by end of the month, a number of Chatos deployed to Malaga to participate in the battle for that city. On 1 February, Squadron Leader Anton Kovalieski, alias "Casimiro," was killed in his I-15 and on 16 February, the American volunteer pilot, Frank G. Tinker of the ***Lacalle*** Squadron was shot up in the battle of Jarama, crash landed and was injured. He later rejoined the squadron. During the conflict he scored a total of eight kills and was one of the few non-Soviet pilots who flew both the I-15 and I-16. By the end of February some fifteen I-15s had been lost.

On 8 July, a Messerschmitt Bf-109 was shot down by an I-15 of the 1st Squadron. Messerschmitt Bf-109 pilots were warned to treated the ***Chato*** with respect and to avoid close combat. On 13 July the American volunteer, Harold "Diaz Evans" Dahl, an ace with five kills, was shot down. He was captured by the Nationalist and remained in a Spanish prison until 1940, when he was allowed to return to the United States. After the end of the Second World War he became a pilot for the Swiss airline Swissair. On 26 July, a Junkers Ju-52 was shot down by I-15s followed by a second on 15 September.

A ground crewman refuels the Spanish-built I-15 (CA-142) of Vicente Castillo, 1st Escuadrilla at Monjos during December of 1938. This unit was mainly used in the ground attack role. CA-142 was manufactured at Molins and left the factory on 24 July 1938. (Museo del Aire)

On 2 November 1938, during the final stages of the battle of Ebro, *Sargento* (Sergeant) Arranz of the 4th Escuadrilla defected with his Spanish-built I-15 (CA-108) to the Nationalist side. CA-108 was built at Sabadell and left the factory on 23 June 1938. Shortly after landing at La Cenia, the Soviet fighter was inspected by German personnel of the Legion Condor. (Museo del Aire)

January 1938 was not without its price, and no less than fourteen I-15s were lost. On 21 February 1938, two I-15s were shot down in the Teruel zone, two were destroyed in accidents and seven in bombing raids. By the end of February there were only thirty-three remaining.

In March of 1938, twenty I-15s were lost, but a victory was claimed on 20 March, when a Fiat BR.20 was shot down by I-15s. In April, no losses were reported and in late May eight I-15s were lost, but due to the deliveries of locally manufactured I-15s, the ***Fuerza Aereas Republicanas*** still had some fifty ***Chatos*** in service. This figure rose to 104 by August. By this time, the ***Chatos*** found themselves hopelessly outnumbered and forced to change bases frequently, often operating from narrow valleys and almost within sight of the ever-retreating front. Due to is sturdy design and four guns, the I-15 was also well suited for ground attack duties. In March of 1937, a combination of bad weather and resolute ground strafing stopped the Italian ***Corpo Truppi Voluntari*** (Volunteer Corps) motorized divisions as they tried to cut off Madrid from the north-east.

As air operations continued into 1938, Soviet losses mounted into the hundreds and air superiority was lost. By Summer, it was no longer an effective force and the Kremlin ordered a withdrawal. By the end of the year, all Soviet personnel had returned home. When they departed, they left the Spanish Republicans what remained of their aircraft. But precious little was left, of the 1,400 aircraft supplied to Spain between October of 1936 and the end of 1938, some 1,176 - or 83 per cent, had been destroyed.

In January of 1939, there were only eighteen I-15s operational at Catalonia. In February ten damaged aircraft were set on fire by the Republicans to prevent from them falling into enemy hands. On 7 February the Nationalists captured twenty-two damaged ***Chatos*** at Tortella.

When the war ended, two squadrons surrendered at Barajas on 29 March 1939 and five I-15s escaped to Algeria in North Africa. A day later, twenty unserviceable I-15s were captured at San Javier airfield and, on 31 March 1939, the Republic surrendered to Franco's Junta.

Spanish-built I-15s

In February of 1937, the Commander in Chief of the Soviet air component in Spain, Colonel Yakob Shmushkievich, submitted a proposal to build the I-15 under license in Spain. ***Construcciones Aeronauticas, S.A.*** (CASA), founded during 1923, had maintained high standards in the aviation industry and it was felt the company would be able to meet all the requirements for a license production program for the I-15. The original schedule called for the first completed I-15 to be rolled off the assembly line on 1 May 1937. The plan called for nine production batches, for a total of 300 ***Chatos***. Initially, the ***Servicio de Aviacion y Fabrication*** plant (SAF-3), at Reus (Tarragona) in Catalania was tasked with building the airframe, while the M-25 power plant, armament and part of the instrumentation, would be imported from the Soviet Union. The parts imported from the Soviet Union were purchased in cash or gold on a US-Dollar basis.

SAF-16, established in a former weaving-mill at Sabadell, was initially intended to only manufacturer components for the I-15, but later, SAF-16 built full aircraft for the Republican forces. Late in the Spanish civil war, additional production facilities were set up at Molins and Villafranca.

The first Spanish manufactured I-15 (CA-001) left the factory on 21 July 1937. While all Soviet supplied I-15s carried the lettering "CC" (*Caza Chato/Chato* fighter) on the fuselage,

Spanish Trainer Modifications

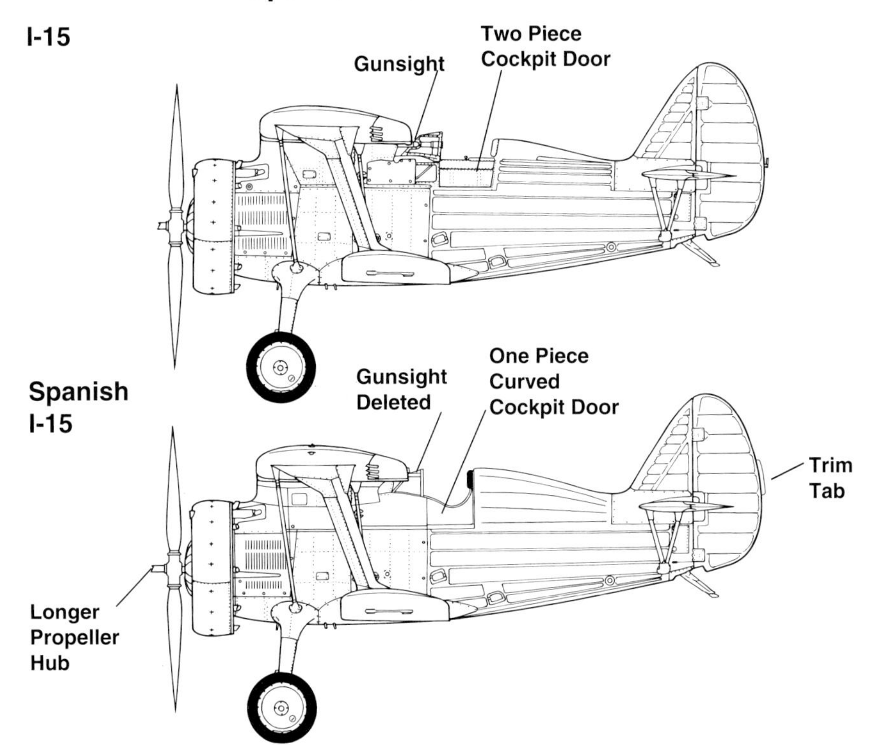

A I-15 trainer, Black 8-21, parked on the dirt ramp at Sabadell on 23 July 1941. The two piece cockpit side doors were replaced by a single curved door and the PV-1 machine guns and OP-1 gunsight had been removed. The aircraft was also modified with a large trim tab on the rudder. (Museo del Aire)

all Spanish built fighters received a "CA" (***Construcciones Aeronauticas***/Aviation Industry) code. The first batch of seventy-five I-15s produced at Reus, Sabadell, Molins and Villafranca were delivered by May of 1938. These were followed by a second batch of fifty Chatos. The third batch included twenty-five aircraft, but on its ferry flight, CA-145 was damaged and subsequently captured. Five aircraft of Lot 4 were also damaged before they reached the combat units, while all twenty-five ***Chatos*** of Batch 5 were built and delivered.

Due to the fact that Nationalist Forces had overran the Sabadell production plant, only sixteen aircraft of Batch 6 could be delivered, while nine airframes fell into the hands of the enemy forces. In the 7th and last batch, only eleven I-15 were produced at Molins and only ten additional C***hatos*** could be manufactured before the Nationalist forces occupied these two production plants.

None of the fighters in Lot 8 and Lot 9 were actually built, but a number of airframes in various stages of constructions were captured by Franco's troops. In total, 231 of the 300 1-15s scheduled to built in Spain were completed at the following locations: Reus (60), Sabadell (83), Molins (67) and Villafranca (21).

The aim to produce at least two I-15s a day was never archived and there were significant differences in output of the Spanish production line during the civil war. In January 1938, a monthly output of fourteen was achieved. In February, only four were produced, but in March another twelve I-15s left the production lines. Difficulties in the supply of M-25 engines were compounded throughout 1938 by shortages of propellers, guns and raw materials. Due to the advancing Nationalist Forces, production came to a halt in January 1939.

There were some differences between the Spanish and Soviet produced I-15s. Additionally, when the Soviet produced aircraft went in for major overhauls, some features typical on Spanish-built I-15s were retrofitted to the Soviet built aircraft. Based on combat experience a sheet of contoured armor-plating for the pilot's seat, capable of withstanding hits form the 12.7MM Breda-Sarfat machine guns of the CR.32, was introduced on Spanish-built aircraft.

A Polikarpov I-15, 8-164, of the *Ejercito del Aire* (Spanish Air Force) at Barajas Airfield near Madrid in 1941. This *Chato* has been modified with a I-16 type spinner and a small trim tab fitted on each upper wing aileron. (Juan Arraez Cerda)

The electric starter in the I-15 was deleted because of weight, being replaced by the use of Hucks lorry. This took longer than self-starting, and a number of I-15s were lost in surprise attacks before they could get airborne.

This I-15 (Black 32-2) carries the post war markings of the *Ejercito del Aire* (Spanish Air Force) . The aircraft was assigned to *Regimiento de Caza 32* (Fighter Regiment 32) based at San Javier (Murcia). The trim tab on the rudder, curved single piece cockpit door and I-16 spinner were all features introduced on the *Chato* at the end of the Spanish civil war. (Juan Arraez Cerda)

Some I-15s were also modified with the modern ShKAS 7.62MM gun imported from the Soviet Union, replacing the standard PV-1 machine guns. The ShKAS was the same caliber as the PV-1, but had an improved rate of fire of 1,800 rpm (from 780 rpm on the PV-1). Besides this advantage, the ShKAS was lighter, and could be selectively fired, that is, the pilot could choose to fire one, two, three or all four guns.

Some I-15 equipped with the initial M-22 power plant were upgraded with M-25 engines taken from damaged I-16s. These were assigned to privileged pilots; such as Squadron Leaders and very experienced pilots, who could get the best results from the improved ***Chato***.

Some ***Chatos*** were used for night fighter missions during the Spanish civil war. These were given a ring manifold connecting all the exhaust stubs, directing the exhaust under the aircraft. By redirecting the exhaust, the pilot's night vision was maintained. A number of modified aircraft were allocated to the ***Escuadrilla de Caza Nocturna*** (Night Fighter Squadron).

When the Nationalist captured the remaining I-15s , they continued to use them in the trainer role, and additional changes were introduced. A large trim tab was added to the rudder and a few also had a small trim tab added to the upper wing aileron. These aircraft also had their armament deleted and the windscreen modified.

The two piece port side cockpit access door and the single piece starboard side cockpit door were both replaced by a single piece curved door with a leather covering for enhanced pilot comfort. This modification was introduced after a number of complaints from pilots that the side doors, designed for cold climates, compressed the pilot, making lateral movement and exiting the aircraft more difficult.

Most postwar I-15s were also modified with I-16 type propellers. This feature could be identified by the more elongated propeller hub. The M-22 power plant on early Chatos was replaced by the M-25 engine, found in vast numbers in the country, this stock being added to by equipment returned by the French government after the end of the civil war.

Experimental I-15s

NACA Cowling

One pre-production I-15 was fitted with a NACA type cowling ring around the Wright SGR-1820 F-3 Cyclone radial engine to determine if this type of cowl ring would reduce drag and improve performance. In the event, this modification was not approved for production.

Conventional Wing Center Section

In spite of the advantages the I-15 had over other contemporary fighters, the Chaika wing had not gained wide spread approval from service pilots. There were arguments and Polikarpov was forced to return to the standard biplane configuration, even though he was personally against it.

During early 1935, the engineers of State Aircraft Factory 39 converted a standard I-15 to the traditional straight center wing section. This wing configuration subsequently became standard on the I-15s successor, the I-152. In contrast to the I-152, the upper wing support struts were much stronger and had a much larger diameter. The starboard upper wing also mounted a rear view mirror.

The first converted I-15 was ready for flight testing in March of 1935. During the trials, no

This pre-production I-15 was equipped with a NACA type engine cowling for experimental purposes. The two fairings on starboard wing tip were only used on pre-production I-15s. (Ivan Ivanow)

national markings or tactical numbers were carried on the aircraft. The results gained with the 'straight' wing I-15 experimental aircraft subsequently lead to the TsKB-3bis prototype.

High Altitude I-15

Polikarpov and his team were anxious to add to the laurels that they had acquired with their fighters and, despite the fact the Soviet Union was not a member of the FIA, so any records would not be recognized internationally, set their sights on establishing a new altitude record. On 21 November 1935, test pilot Vladimir K. Kokkinaki set a new world altitude record of 47,818 feet (14,575 meters) with a highly modified I-15. The aircraft was stripped of any equipment not absolutely necessary, including the engine cowling and the fabric covering was unpainted to further reduce weight.

Pressured Cabin I-15GK

Another experimental version of the I-15 was the I-15GK (GK=***Germeticheskij Kabina***/Pressure Cabin) which was equipped with pressurized cabin, made of riveted D1 steel with a rubber sealing. The fuselage was modified with a welded truss frame work with a semi circular fully enclosed canopy. The front windshield was modified to blend into the canopy

This I-15 was modified during March of 1935 at State Aircraft Factory 39, with a conventional wing center in place of the standard gull shaped wing center section. This wing became standard on the I-152 fighter. (Ivan Ivanow)

This heavily modified I-15 captured a new world altitude record of 47,818 feet (14,575 meters) on 21 November 1935, flown by test pilot V. K. Kokkinaki. The device on the wing was part of the test instrumentation. All unnecessary weight, including the engine cowling was removed for the record attempt. (Hans-Joachim Mau)

cover and the rear fabric covered dorsal spine was replaced by a glazed section.

The Type SK-IV cabin added some 100.6 pounds (45.6 kg) to the weight of the I-15. Tests of the I-15GK were flown by Stepan P. Suprun at the Zhukovsky Test and Experimental center during 1937. A year later the pressurized cockpit was modified for armament tests and while the air supply system worked well, the cockpit windows became damp and escape from the aircraft in the event of an emergency proved to be extremely difficult.

I-15GK Pressure Cabin

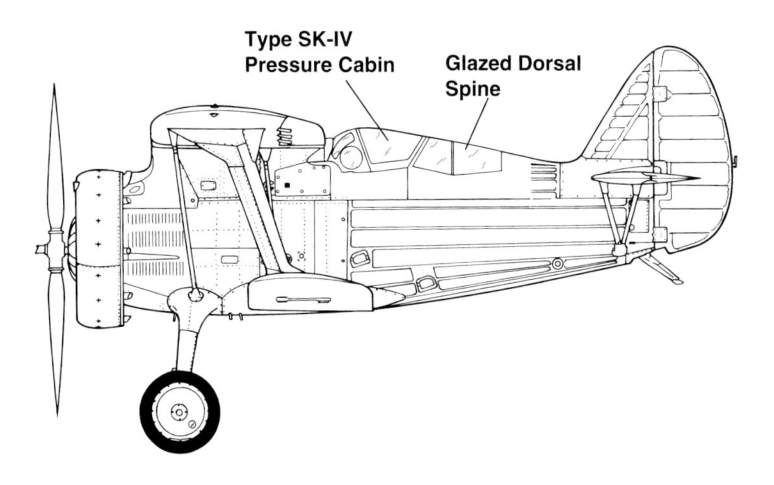

TsKB-3bis Prototype

After the gull winged I-15 entered service, a number of complaints were received from service pilots in front-line units of the Soviet Air Force. These complaints centered around the gull wing itself and they led Polikarpov (even though he was personally opposed to the idea) to design a successor for the I-15 that featured a standard upper wing, with a straight center section and interplane N struts, under the designation TsKB-3bis.

The TsKB-3bis prototype would be powered by 775 hp M-25V power plant, a progressive improvement of the M-25 (Wright-Cyclone). This modified power plant had a K-25-4D carburetor and some minor internal improvements. The empty weight of the engine rose from 959 pounds (435 kg) to 1,012 pounds (459 kg).

The TsKB-3bis prototype differed from a standard I-15 in a number of ways besides the new upper wing configuration. An aerodynamically clean, long-chord cowling replaced the Townend ring. This cowling incorporated a baffle plate with adjustable cooling shutters in front of the engine. The exhaust system was modified to include a collector ring and a single large exhaust port on each side of the nose. A cooling air scoop was added to the top of the cowling ring. The prototype also featured streamlined wheel pants over the main wheels in an effort to lessen drag. The TsKB-3bis had a tail wheel in place of the tail-skid used on the production I-15.

The triangle shaped windscreen of the I-15 was replaced by a frameless, rounded windscreen, which was similar to that used on the I-16 monoplane fighter. The OP-1 gunsight used on all production I-15s was replaced by an improved PAK-1 gunsight (which was a copy of the French Clair gunsight). The TsKB-3bis prototype was equipped with a RSI-3 radio with antenna stubs mounted on each wing tip. The antenna wires ran from the wing tip masts to a small mast mounted on the front of the fin. While some of the standard production I-15s had each a position light on top and bottom of the upper wing tip, the TsKB-3bis and all subsequent I-152 production aircraft had a single position light on the outer wing tip. There was also a rear view mirror fitted on the starboard upper wing of the TsKB-3bis

A small window was added to the fuselage dorsal spine, just behind the headrest. While the production Soviet I-15 had no trim tab on the rudder, the TsKB-3bis and all I-152s had a large trim tab on the rudder, with a position light fitted on the rudder. Additionally, the prototype had trim tabs on the elevators, a feature not found on the I-15.

The first TsKB-3bis prototype was equipped with a RSI-3 radio. The antenna masts were mounted on both wing upper surfaces near the wing tip. The vertical fin was smaller then on the late production I-152. (Ivan Ivanow)

The TsKB-3bis prototype was equipped with a windscreen similar to that used on the I-16 and a PAK-1 gun sight. The window in the dorsal spine behind the cockpit was deleted on production I-152s. (Zdenek Hurt)

Polikarpov I-152

Although the I-152 was equipped with the more powerful M-25V engine, some areas of its performance was actually below that of the I-15. The I-15 could reach 16,405 feet (5,000 meter) in 6.1 minutes, while the I-152 took 6.7 minutes. Service ceiling was reduced from 32,152 feet (9,800 meters) to 30,511 feet (9,300 meters). One of the reasons behind this decrease in performance was the fact that the I-152 was built stronger than the I-15 and the empty weight had gone up by 771.6 pounds (350 kg). The I-152 was faster in level flight and in a dive than the I-15, but it was far inferior in dogfighting maneuvers. Its ground handling and the pilot's visibility during take-off was better than the I-15s, due to the traditional biplane wing configuration. But, once airborne, most I-152 pilots complained that the aircraft's agility and sensitivity was inferior to the I-15.

The I-152 went into full production during the Autumn of 1937 at GAZ-21, followed by GAZ-1 at Khodinka. When production was finally phased out during early 1939, some 2,408 aircraft had left the production line.

There were a number of differences between the TsKB-3bis prototype and production I-152s. The cowling of the production I-152 was outfitted with adjustable cooling shutters. While the prototype was equipped with a PAK-1 gunsight, the I-152 reverted to the OP-1 gunsight as used on the I-15. The windscreen was replaced with a more rounded type, better suited for mass production.

The rear view mirror mounted on the starboard upper wing of the TsKB-3bis was deleted on the I-152, as were the small windows on the dorsal spine behind the cockpit. While the TsKB-3bis prototype had a straight cockpit door ledge, the I-152 had a slightly curved ledge. A section of 9MM armor plate was added behind the pilots seat, a feature based on combat experience with the I-15 in Spain.

The TsKB-3bis prototype was fitted with a radio and antenna masts, while most I-152s did not have the radio or antenna masts on the upper wing surfaces. The few I-152s which had radios could be identified by a small radio antenna mast fitted on top of the fin; however, there was no radio masts installed on the upper wing.

The TsKB-3bis prototype was equipped with a tail wheel, but production I-152s reverted to the traditional tail skid, which was larger on early production I-152s. Later, the skid was reduced in size to one very similar to that used on the I-15.

The TsKB-3bis had a smaller fin and rudder with a more pointed tip, while production I-

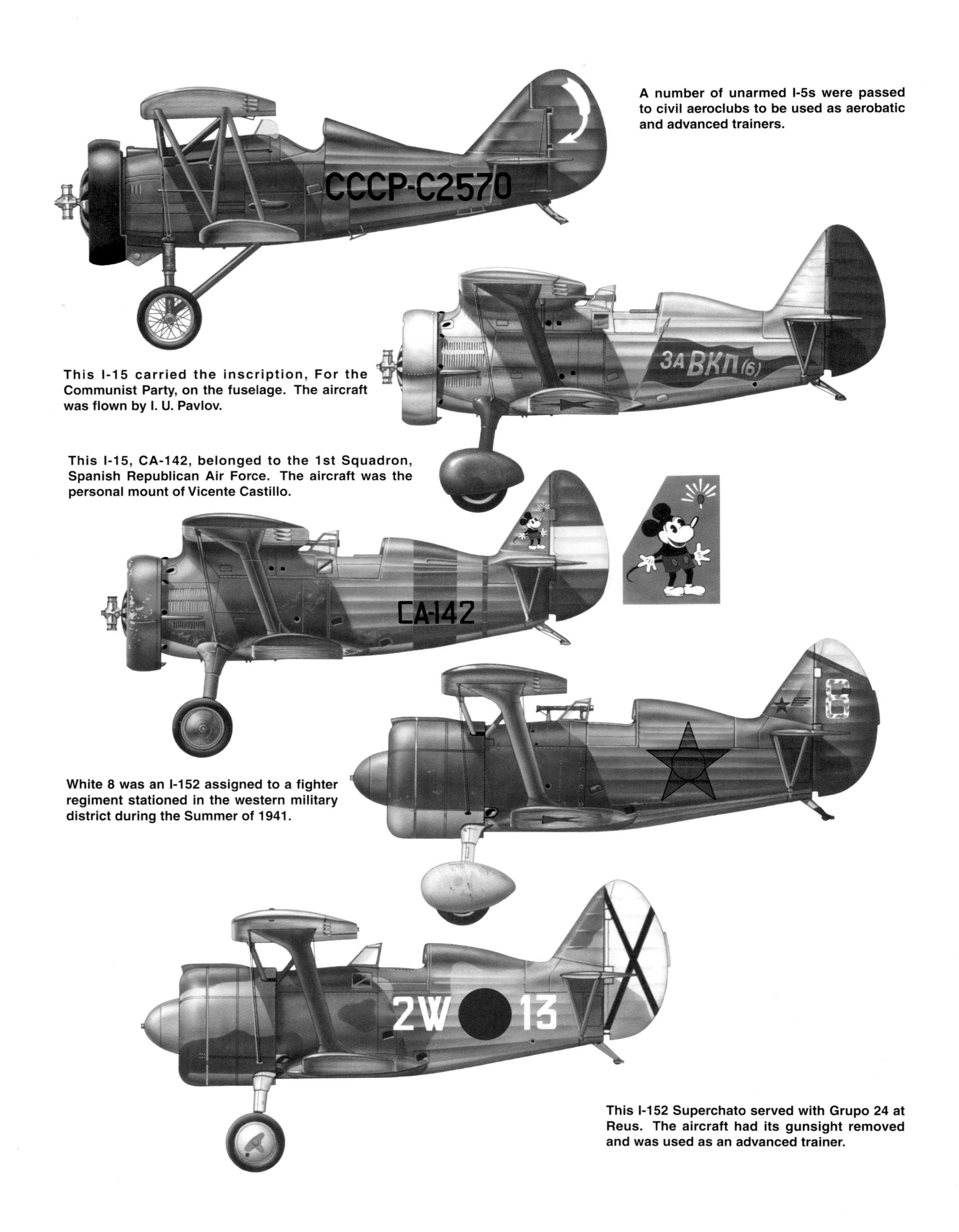

A number of unarmed I-5s were passed to civil aeroclubs to be used as aerobatic and advanced trainers.

This I-15 carried the inscription, For the Communist Party, on the fuselage. The aircraft was flown by I. U. Pavlov.

This I-15, CA-142, belonged to the 1st Squadron, Spanish Republican Air Force. The aircraft was the personal mount of Vicente Castillo.

White 8 was an I-152 assigned to a fighter regiment stationed in the western military district during the Summer of 1941.

This I-152 Superchato served with Grupo 24 at Reus. The aircraft had its gunsight removed and was used as an advanced trainer.

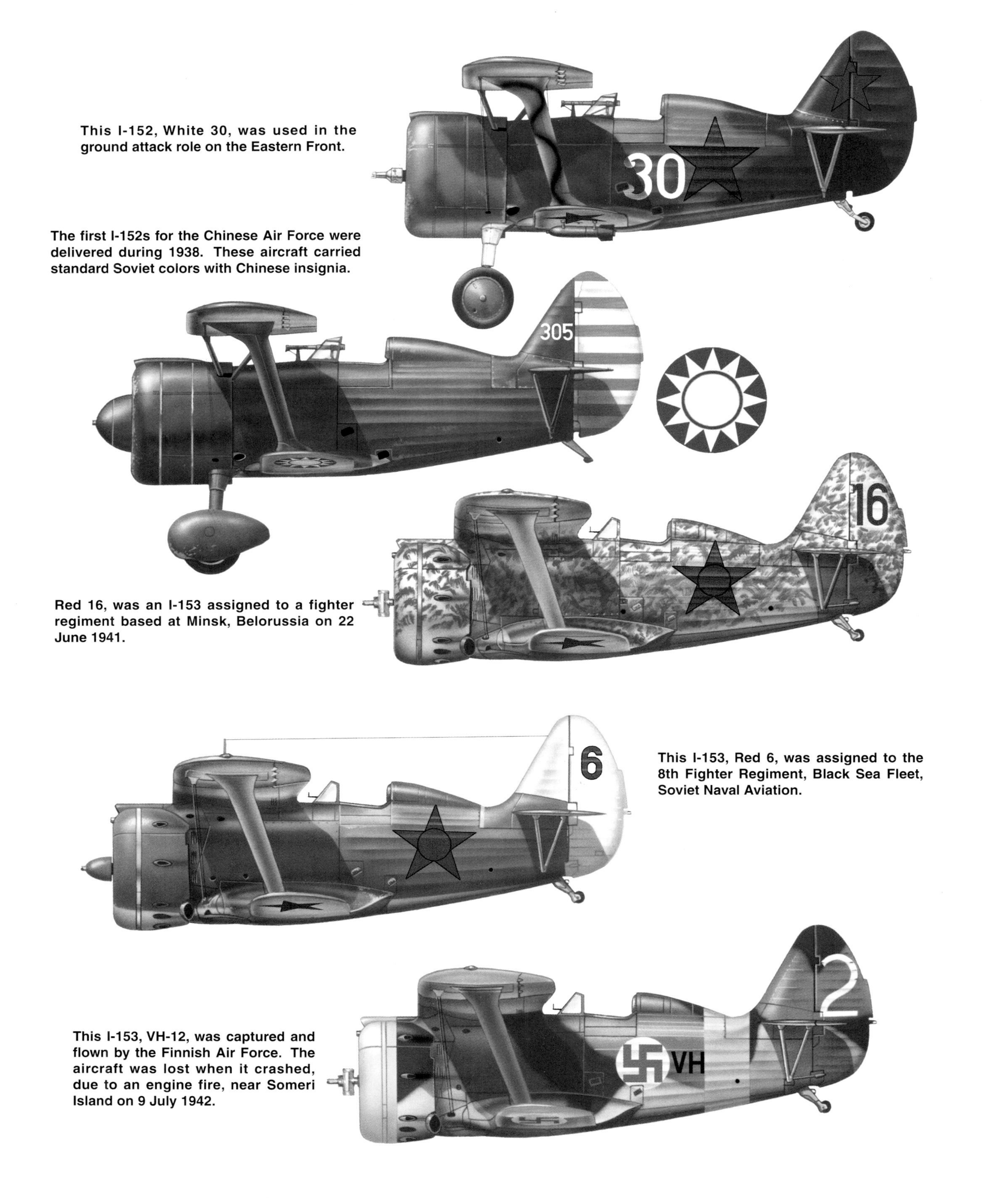

This I-152, White 30, was used in the ground attack role on the Eastern Front.

The first I-152s for the Chinese Air Force were delivered during 1938. These aircraft carried standard Soviet colors with Chinese insignia.

Red 16, was an I-153 assigned to a fighter regiment based at Minsk, Belorussia on 22 June 1941.

This I-153, Red 6, was assigned to the 8th Fighter Regiment, Black Sea Fleet, Soviet Naval Aviation.

This I-153, VH-12, was captured and flown by the Finnish Air Force. The aircraft was lost when it crashed, due to an engine fire, near Someri Island on 9 July 1942.

Wing Development

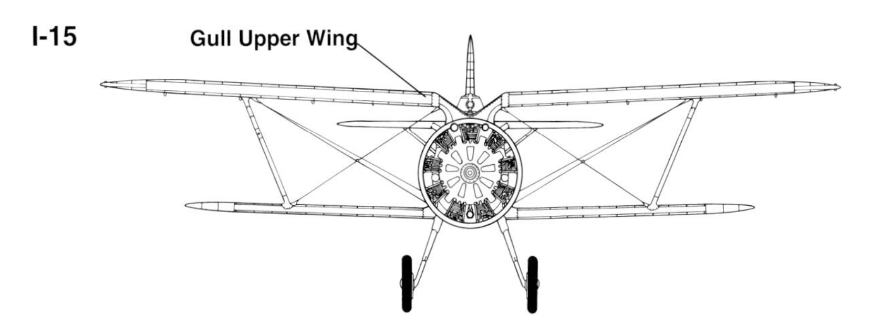

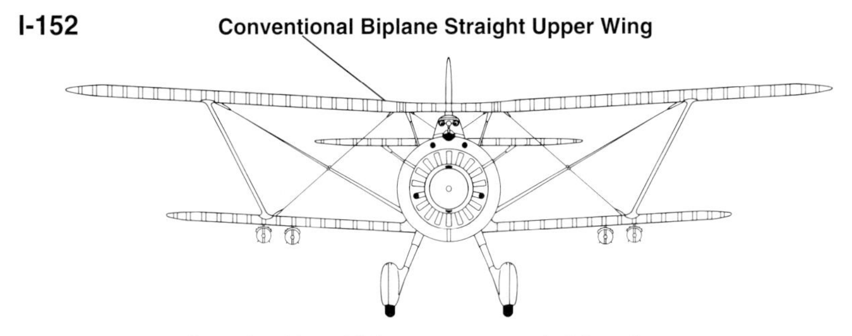

152s had a taller fin and rudder which was more rounded than the prototype.

The armament of the I-152 remained the same as the I-15, four PV-1 7.62MM machine guns. The TsKB-3bis prototype had no provision for external armament, but all I-152s could mount two bomb racks under each lower wing for up to 330 pounds (150 kg) of ordnance. These racks could carry two 110 pound (50 kg), four 55 pound (25 kg) or eight 22 pound (10 kg) bombs. Bomb types included the AO-10, the AO-20M or FAB-50M bombs, or ChAB-25, the AOCh-15 chemical weapons. Instead of the bombs, two 21 gallon (80 liter) fuel tanks could be a carried on the same racks. The four bomb racks could also be replaced by four Type RO

This pre-production I-152 was tested by the Scientific Research Institute of the Soviet Air Force. The aircraft carried no markings other than a White 68 which was crudely painted on the vertical fin. (Robert Bock)

An early production I-152, Red 5, in flight over the Soviet countryside. The tactical number had a thin White outline. This fighter was equipped with the initial large tailskid. The aircraft was also equipped with a RSI-3 radio, with one of the antenna masts being mounted on the top of the fin. (Viktor Kulikov)

Development

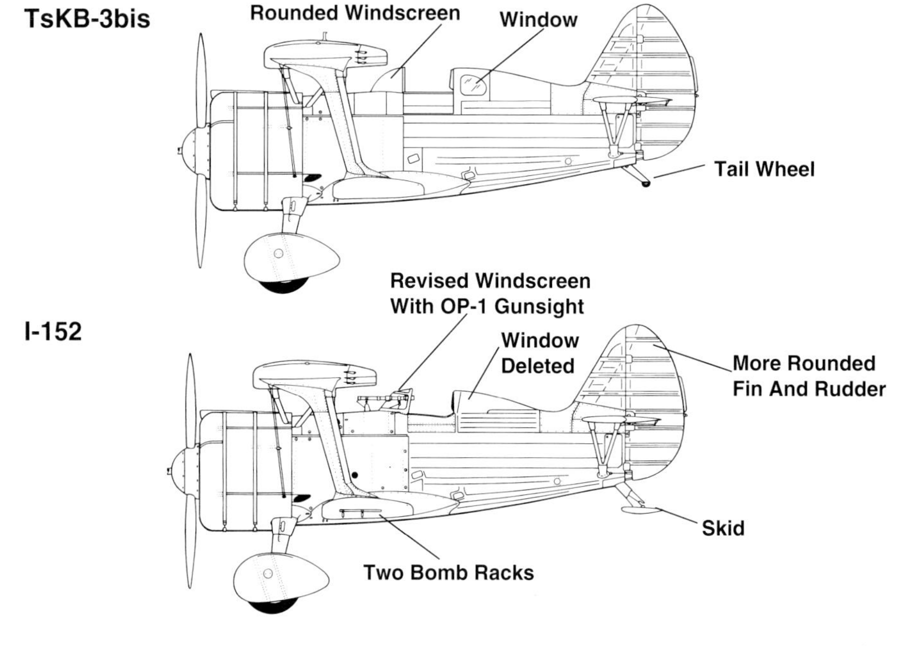

This badly damaged I-152 was captured by Hungarian troops in the Ukraine and taken to Budapest, where was part of an exhibition of Soviet war booty held in May of 1942 in the Hungarian capital. The aircraft was missing many items, including the ailerons which had been removed by trophy hunters. (Odon Horvath)

rocket rails capable of launching the RS-82 unguided air-to-ground rocket.

During normal front-line operations during the Great Patriotic War, most combat Regiments removed the main wheel pants and the spinner over the V-25 propeller. There were also various types of ski landing gears used during the Winter months. In most cases the skis were fixed with belts leading to the fuselage and the engine cowling. Another front-line modification was that the standard tail skid was often replaced by the tail wheel used I-153. These tail-

This I-152, Red 8, was captured by the advancing Wehrmacht on the Russian Front and marked with a Yellow Swastika on the fin. This I-152 was unusual in that the spinner was painted Light Blue and the outer half of the port wing undersurface was in Olive Green. (Henry Hoppe)

One of the many I-152 captured nearly intact during the initial days of the German invasion. The OP-1 gunsight was removed for study. The tip of the fin was in Yellow and the aircraft carried a Red winged star on the vertical fin and a White 8 on the rudder. (Heinz Birkholz)

wheels were obtained from wrecked I-153s.

Most I-152s were delivered from the factory with Olive Drab uppersurfaces and Light Blue undersurfaces. At this time, a considerable amount of the paint used in the Soviet aviation industry was imported from Germany and, as a result, the colors applied to Soviet pre-war fighters were very similar to those used on German aircraft. Until the Summer of 1941, the national markings were applied to the top of upper wing and under the lower wing, as well on the fuselage. At this time, the Red star had a small Black circle within the Star and a thin Black outline. The interplane struts were usually painted in Light Blue, although some examples had the interplane struts in a Dark Olive Green. The tactical number was usually applied to the rudder and had a thin White outline. There were several variations of tactical numbers used in different I-152 fighter regiments.

When the Great Patriotic War (the Second World War) started on 22 June 1941, there were a number of I-152 painted in a two tone camouflage scheme. Some aircraft carried an Olive Green/Light Green pattern, others an Olive Green/Black-Green pattern on the uppersurface over Light Blue undersurfaces. There was no official camouflage guidelines and the colors, now from Soviet manufactured stocks, since the original German paints were exhausted, were sometimes locally manufactured and differed in shade and tone. The Red Star national markings were generally deleted from the wing upper surfaces to aid in the camouflage effect. In addition, the small Black circle within national marking was also deleted. Some aircraft carried a second Red star, with a thin Black outline, on the fin, while the tactical number was moved to the fuselage.

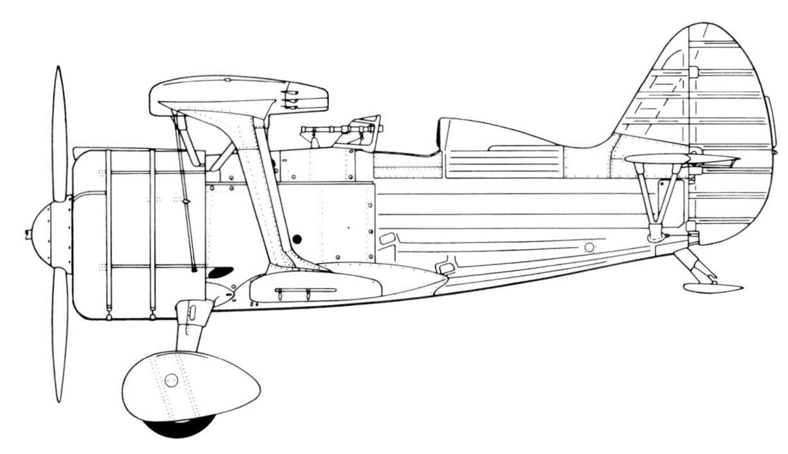

Specification

Polikarpov I-152

Wingspan...33 feet 5.5 inches (10.2 m)
Length..20 feet 7 inches (6.24 m)
Height..9 feet 8 inches (3 m)
Empty Weight..2,888 pounds (1,310 kg)
Maximum Weight....................................4,044 pounds (1,834kg)
Powerplant..One 775 hp Shvetsov M-25V air-cooled radial engine
Armament..Four 7.62MM machine guns
Speed...226 mph (363.7 kph)
Service Ceiling.......................................31,165 feet (9,499 m)
Range...497 miles (800km)
Crew...One

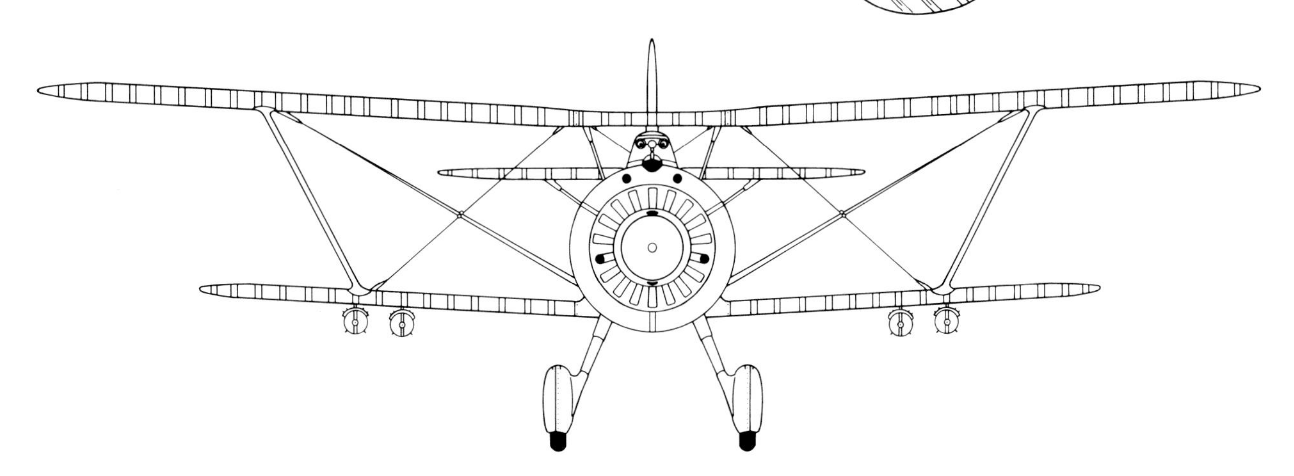

Combat

On 18 September 1931, Japan invaded Manchuria setting up a new state, Manchukno, with a Japanese puppet government. On 12 March 1936, the Soviets signed a mutual assistance pact with the Mongolian People's Republic, giving Japan a clear warning to keep out of Mongolia.

A series of skirmishes between Soviet-Mongolian and Japanese forces on the Manchukuoan-Mongolian border that had begun during 1936, flared into full scale, but undeclared warfare on 11 May 1939. The area of conflict was a strip of arid pasture between the Khalkin-Gol river and the village of Nomonhan. In sheer numbers, the armies and air forces engaged in the fighting were greater even than those in the Spanish Civil War. To command Soviet air operations, the High Command dispatched Yakob Smushkievich, former Commander in Chief of the Soviet air contingent in Spain, to the battle zone.

The I-152 regiment, under the command of Major V.M. Zabaluev, soon found itself opposed in combat over the Nomonhan plateau by Nakajima Type 97 monoplane fighters. The air activity over Mongolia was quite hectic, and engagements involving 90 to 100 aircraft becoming common place. On 22 June 1939, some 95 I-152s and I-16s fighters engaged over 120 Japanese aircraft. When the engagement finished thirty-four Japanese and fourteen Soviet aircraft had been lost.

Obviously, the experience gained over China and especially Mongolia, showed that despite organized mutual support between the maneuverable I-152 and the I-16, the combat capability of the former, with its relatively low speed, could not match modern Japanese fighters. The I-152s performance deficit prevented Soviet pilots from dictating their own tactics when in combat with the Japanese monoplanes.

Although outclassed when the Germans invaded the Soviet Union on Sunday, 22 June 1941, the I-152 was actively engaged in combat on the Eastern front. On the first day, the German Luftwaffe destroyed no less than 1,489 Soviet aircraft on the ground. These aircraft had been deployed to forward Soviet airfields in the Ukraine, Latvia, Estonia and Lithuania. A substantial number of these were Polikarpov fighters. With their loss, Soviet Air Force ceased to exist

An abandoned I-152 found on an Ukrainian airfield by advancing German troops during the Summer of 1941. Undamaged Soviet fighters found by German troops had the OP-1 gunsight quickly removed to prevent them from being used, this became a common practice among German forces. This aircraft carried no tactical number. (Frieder Voigt)

During the German surprise attack to the Soviet Union on 22 June 1941, there were many Soviet fighters parked on open airfields that were put out of action by four-pound SD-2 fragmentation bombs. On the first day of Operation BARBAROSSA, some 1,489 aircraft were destroyed on the ground. (ECPA DAA-1093 L-10)

This overall Light Gray I-152 was used as a static demonstrator at a German Naval station. Part of the fuselage panels as well the OP-1 gunsight are missing and the *Balkenkreuz* was crudely applied to the fuselage. (Bundesarchive)

During the winter, many I-152 were equipped with ski landing gear, like White 17. The engine cowling shutters are all closed to help keep the engine from freezing. This aircraft is equipped with two bomb racks under each lower outer wing panel. (Keski-Suomen Ilmailumuseo via Hannu Valtonen)

as a threat to German air superiority.

The I-152s served mainly in the ground support role, although few were used as pure fighters. Its diving ability, armor and extraordinary structural strength made it a good attack plane. Most of the I-152s destroyed during the early Luftwaffe attacks in the Ukraine, Polish occupied territory and Baltic districts, were assigned to Assault Regiments within the Soviet Air Force.

One of the I-152 units which fought on the Eastern front was the 653rd Regiment. It was established in December of 1941 at the aviation school at Rehev. After a brief training period, the unit was declared operational in the Crimea sector on the Black Sea. Although it was nominally a fighter regiment, it mainly served in the fighter-bomber/assault role. Before the regiment went into action, the main problem faced by the ground crews was to adapt the I-152 for strike missions, since the aircraft had no bomb sight.

One of the pilots suggested putting two lines on the windscreen. Pilots used these lines during dive bombing. Bombs were dropped when a distance between the lines concluded with the size of a target. There were jokers in the Regiment who said, "It would be better if we

Sergeant I.P. Guborev of the 11th Fighter Regiment in front of his camouflged I-152, White 86, at Ladoga during 1942. (Keski-Suomen Ilmailumuseo via Hannu Valtonen)

Senior Lieutenant V.F. Abramov of the 11th Fighter Aviation Regiment takes off for a ground attack mission during 1942. The I-152 was armed with a pair of RS-82 unguided air-to-ground rockets under each wing. The aircraft has been modified with the tailwheel from a I-153 in place of the standard I-152 tailskid. (Zdenek Hurt)

This I-152, Yellow 68, was camouflaged with a two tone upper surface scheme of Olive Green and Dark Green. It carried late style national markings, of the type not introduced before early 1944. The aircraft was armed with RO rocket rails for RS-82 rockets under each wing. (A.A. Zirnov)

The OP-1 was gunsight used on the I-15 and I-152. The open fuselage panel reveals part of the upper PV-1 7.62MM machine gun and shell ejector chute. (Keski-Suomen Ilmailumuseo via Hannu Valtonen)

The relatively rudimentary cockpit instrumentation of a I-152 with flight instruments being grouped in the center panel. The Black handle at the right below the cockpit rim was the charging handle for the upper 7.62MM machine gun. (Keski-Suomen Ilmailumuseo via Hannu Valtonen)

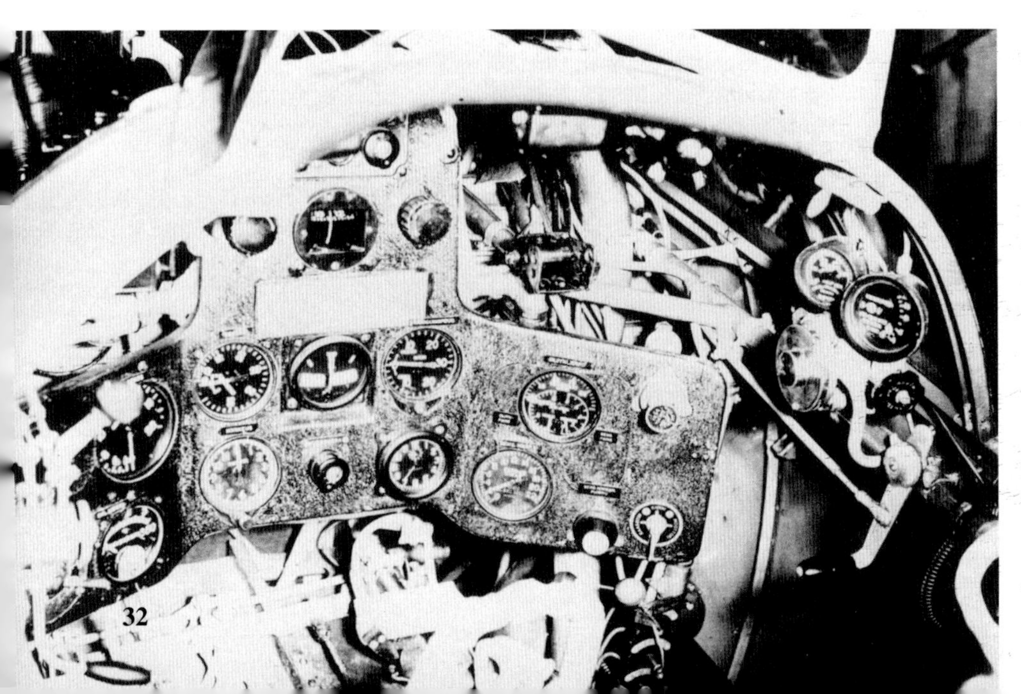

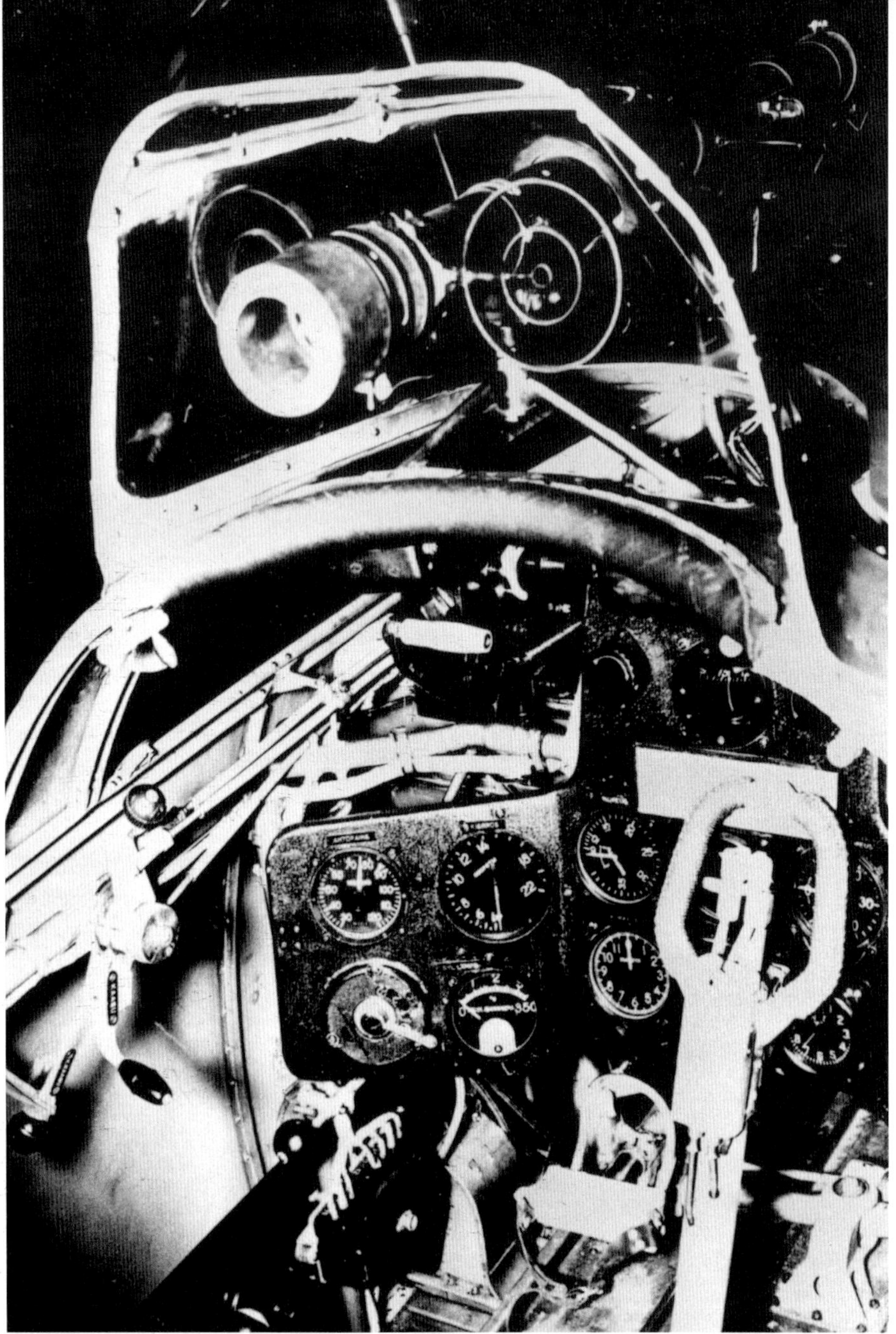

The I-152 had a typical cockpit layout with rather simple and rudimentary cockpit instrumentation. Most Soviet pilots; however, reportedly found the accuracy of the instruments to be quite good. (Keski-Suomen Ilmailumuseo via Hannu Valtonen)

This I-152 was used during the Great Patriotic War (Second World War) in the assault/ground attack role with two RS-82 air-to-ground rockets fitted under each wing. The spinner and wheel pants were removed, a common feature of ground support I-152s. (G.F. Petrov)

borrowed a sling from our ancestors." But, since it was clear that no bomb-sight would be supplied by a factory, there was no other way. The question then became, where to place the lines on the canopy, at what distance should the target be when between the lines and what dive angle should be maintained? To find the answers, the two sections within the Regiments were formed to test the concepts and develop tactics. The first section was comprised of experienced pilots and the second element was made up of pilots of average skill.

While the I-15 had individual exhaust stacks, the I-152 had an exhaust collector ring with a single large exhaust stack on each side of the fuselage. The fuel tank is visible just behind the firewall. (Keski-Suomen Ilmailumuseo via Hannu Valtonen)

The lower port PV-1 7.62MM machine gun. The lower guns were fitted with barrel extensions that ran through the engine cylinders. The large removable maintenance panels made maintenance in the field far easier, even under austere conditions. (Keski-Suomen Ilmailumuseo via Hannu Valtonen)

The I-152 was fitted with a V-25 propeller which was driven by the M-25V radial engine. The engine shutters could be opened or closed depending on the weather conditions. The blast tubes for the upper machine guns are visible above the engine , and one of the lower gun blast tubes is visible just below the propeller blade at the left. (Keski-Suomen Ilmailumuseo via Hannu Valtonen)

First, the pilots tried to find correct distance between lines at an angle of diving of 45 degrees. During the early flights, marks were placed in the canopy and bombs then dropped from 1,968 feet (600 meters), but results were not very accurate. Later, the distance between the lines was changed and the I-152s dropped their loads from 656 feet (200 meters) with far better results.

Later, each pilot worked out the most comfortable dive angle and distance for himself. Additionally, the pilots had to develop tactics for using RS-82 unguided rockets. On his first combat sortie with the RS-82, V. Kubaniev destroyed a Messerschmitt Bf-109 with these rockets. The 653rd Fighter Regiment used the I-152 until June of 1942, although there were a number of ground attack regiments which used the I-152 well into 1943.

A single Naval Regiment of the Northern Fleet was equipped with the I-152 as a first-line fighter. This was the 72nd Combined Regiment, which had twenty-eight I-152s on strength. Until mid-July of that same year, this was the only Soviet Naval fighter outfit and it saw combat operations over the Kola Peninsula. The I-152 was also used by a Naval Regiment of the Black Sea Fleet, the 8th Fighter Regiment at Kacha Airfield near Sevastopol.

Chinese I-152s

During the civil war in China, the Kuonmintang Party under Sun Yat-Sen, established contact with the Soviet Union. In January of 1934, Japanese troops attacking northern China moving through the Mongolian People's Republic, causing a serious military incident. On 7 July 1937, Japan began its full-scale invasion of China, without a declaration of war.

On 21 August 1937, a non-aggression pact had been signed between the Soviet Union and the Chinese Central Government and, under the terms of one of the secret clauses, the Soviet Union was to send military aid to China. Emphasis was placed on the re-equipment of the Chinese Air Force, which had been virtually annihilated by the Japanese.

During October of 1937, some 450 Soviet pilots and technicians arrived via train at Alma Ata in Kazakhstan, bringing the first of some 225 Soviet aircraft to China. Of these, 115 were fighters, 62 bombers and eight were advanced trainers. These supplies were trucked into China over the old "silk road" to the end of the Chinese railway line at Lanchow.

The I-152 looked to be of the same vintage design as the Curtiss Hawk III, which was first delivered during 1936, but when compared to the American fighter, the I-152 had a number of advantages which were not found in the Curtiss Hawk III. The I-152 was equipped with 9MM of armor plate behind the cockpit seat, the firepower of its four synchronized 7.62MM guns was greater than the two guns on the Curtiss Hawk III. The synchronization gear on the I-152

Chinese Air Force I-152s taxi out for a mission. The national marking was only applied on the under wing surfaces. The I-152 in the foreground carries the tactical number, White 305, on the vertical fin in front of the Blue and White striped rudder. (San Diego Aerospace Museum via Ray Wagner)

This Chinese Air Force I-152 nosed over after a hard landing. The aircraft was modified with a Wright-Cyclone SR-1820-F-53 engine, three blade Hamilton Standard propeller, tail wheel and main landing gear wheels taken from a Curtiss Hawk III. The Chinese Air Force serial number, P.8053, was carried in White on the fin. (San Diego Aerospace Museum via Ray Wagner)

drew interest from American military advisers, and they removed one from a I-152 and shipped it back to the States for evaluation.

Four "volunteer" fighter squadrons, manned by Soviet Air Force personnel, were formed for deployment to China. The fighter element, which was to be led by Stepan P. Suprun, received priority in the supply of the new I-152s. These Soviet formations reached the Nanking area during Autumn of 1937 and were hurriedly committed to battle. They established a degree of air-superiority over the Japanese Imperial Army's Kawasaki Ki-10 biplane, but were easily outclassed by the Japanese Mitsubishi A5M monoplane fighter. The I-152 was faster than the Ki-10 at altitudes up to 11,483 feet (3,500 meters), had a higher rate of climb, and was better armed.

In late 1937, ninety-three I-152 were delivered to the Chinese Central Government, followed by a further ninety-three during the first four months of 1938. The effectiveness of the Chinese fighter squadrons was poor; however, due to the poor standard of Chinese pilot training.

On 18 February 1938, fifteen Japanese bombers, escorted by eleven Mitsubishi A5M fighters attacked the Wuhan area. Nineteen I-152 and ten I-16 of the 4th Group intercepted the attackers. Admitted losses included four Japanese and five Chinese fighter pilots killed in action, including the commander of the 4th Group. Nanchang was the target of thirty-five Mitsubishi G3M2 bombers and eighteen A5M fighters on 25 February 1938, which were met by nineteen I-152s and eleven I-16s. A single Chinese Polikarpov was shot down and a further four made forced landings.

On 15 April 1938, three Japanese Nakajima Ki-27 fighters with twelve Type 95 biplanes fought a pitched battle with thirty Chinese I-152s over Shensi, allegedly destroying no fewer than twenty-four of the Chinese fighters. 29 April 1938, saw the largest air battle of the China war over Wuhan. Eighteen G3M bombers escorted by twenty-seven fighters were met by not less than sixty-seven Polikarpov fighters. Pilots of the Chinese 3rd and 4th Groups had nineteen I-152s and six I-16s, the rest were flown by Soviet airmen. According to Chinese figures, ten Japanese bombers and eleven fighters were shot down for the loss of nine Chinese

This was the result of a collison between a Chinese Vultee V-11 and a I-152. The I-152 was flipped over from the impact, ending up on its back. The V-11 saw action for the first time during the Wuhan campaign. (San Diego Aerospace Museum via Ray Wagner)

planes and four pilots. The Soviets reported two Polikarpov as lost, but their pilots were able to bail out safely.

A Japanese attack on Wuhan on 31 May 1938, was intercepted by thirty-three I-152s and sixteen I-16s, which were flown by thirty-one Soviet and eighteen Chinese pilots. Two Japanese A5M fighters were shot down for the loss of a Soviet I-152 and a Chinese I-16.

Between August of 1937 and October of 1938, when the first phase of the Sino-Japanese war ended, the Chinese Air Force had lost a total of 202 aircraft in combat, with a further 112 damaged. 132 Chinese airmen were reported as killed in action and a further 152 wounded.

During the War of Resistance in 1939, the veteran I-152 and I-16 still served as the backbone of the Chinese Air Force. Except for a dozen Dewoitine D.510s and some Curtiss Hawk 75s, most of the 135 aircraft of the Chinese Air Force were, in fact the obsolete Polikarpov fighter, which had to face about 900 Japanese aircraft.

On 20 February 1939, fifteen Chinese and fourteen Soviet pilots scrambled their I-152s and I-16s, to intercept Japanese bombers which had attacked Lanchow. The Polikarpovs claimed a total of nine victories that day. On 23 February 1939, twelve Japanese bombers were intercepted by twenty-one Chinese and Soviet pilots, and another six Japanese bombers were shot down that day.

In November of 1939, the Soviet volunteer groups began leaving China. Soviet aid had stiffened Chinese resistance against Japan, but the Russians themselves had become "disillusioned and frustrated." They saw their aircraft misused and crashed "by inexperienced Chinese, who would not follow or had not understood the Russian instructions," and saw material being hoarded instead of being used in combat.

The year ended in the Southern Theater of Operations on 30 December 1939, when thirteen Japanese Navy fighters from Nanking challenged a Chinese unit over Liuchow and claimed fourteen I-152s and I-16s downed for one loss.

Without re-equipment or foreign volunteer pilots in 1940, the Chinese had only about 150 aircraft for the whole year. Most of the Japanese Navy bomber force moved up to central China to join the summer strategic bombing offensive against Chungking. On 11 August 1940, ninety Japanese bombers attacking Chungking were intercepted by twenty-nine fighters of the 4th Group using an unique tactic. Six I-152s crossed about sixty-five feet above the bombers path, each releasing four small parachute bombs with six-second fuses. This disrupted the formation, allowing Chinese I-16s to down two and damage other bombers.

On 13 September 1940, the formidable Mitsubishi A6M1 fighter entered combat for the first time over China, when thirteen Zeros escorted twenty-seven G3M2 bombers to Chungking. After the bombers left the target, a Mitsubishi C5M1 reconnaissance aircraft radioed the Japanese fighters that Chinese fighters had been seen at nearby Pi-sham. These included nine I-16s and nineteen I-152 fighters from the 4th Group. The Japanese Zeros surprised them with devastating effect. Thirteen were destroyed, a further eleven damaged with ten Chinese pilots killed and eight, including the 4th Group leader, wounded.

A number of I-152s were locally modified at the Air Force No.1 Aircraft Factory at Gujyang. These I-152s were powered by a Wright-Cyclone SR-1820 F-53 driving a three blade variable pitch Hamilton Standard propeller. These engines and propellers were taken from Curtiss Hawk IIIs. With the new engine, the original cowling of the I-152 was replaced by a shorter engine cowling. The cooling air intake on top of the engine cowling was deleted, as was the shuttered front of the engine cowling. The large exhaust stub on both sides of the original I-152 was replaced by a smaller exhaust stub of a smaller diameter. When the stock of original Soviet tires was exhausted, the I-152 was modified to use tires from the Curtiss Hawk II and Hawk III. The original tail skid was replaced by a tailwheel, with a mud-guard being added in front of the tail wheel.

Chinese Air Force I-152s were all delivered in Soviet Air Force camouflage of Olive Green uppersurfaces and Light Blue undersurfaces. The national marking were carried on the lower wing undersurfaces, but not on the wing upper surface or on the fuselage. The rudder was painted with Blue/White horizontal stripes. Most I-152 carried a White serial number on the tail fin beginning with a P, followed by four digits (for instance P.7179). Some I-152s also carried a three digit White tactical number.

Spanish I-152 "*Superchato*"

Following appeals for more war material from General Hidalgo de Cisneros, the Spanish Commander in Chief of the Republican Air Force, made directly to Stalin, some 250 aircraft of various types shipped via France to Spain. At times, the activities of the Soviet Union

This Spanish I-152 was returned from France after the end of the Civil war. The trim tab on the upper wing aileron was a postwar modification introduced in Spain. The single position light on the wing tip was replaced by two position lights, one on top and one on the bottom of the wing tip. (Museo del Aire)

C-9.8 was the last serviceable *Supercato in* Spanish service. The aircraft served with *Regimiento de Caza 23* at Reus Air Base until 1953. By that time, the aircraft had been repainted with the Red-Yellow-Red Spanish roundel being applied to the fuselage. (Juan Arraez Cerda)

seemed to be as much directed against its allies, Britain and France, as against Franco and the Fascists. Most Soviet officers who were sent to Spain were executed on their return to the Soviet Union, since Stalin feared they had been corrupted by exposure to Western values and could be a threat.

A total of ninety-three crated I-152s were delivered for the ***Fuerza Aereas Republicanas*** (FARE). The I-152s destined for Spain were shipped in three consignments of thirty-one air-

I-152s of the Spanish Air Force all served with *Grupo 24, Regimiento de Caza 23* based at Reus. This particular *Supercato* carried the registration C-9.9 in White on the fin. (Museo del Aire)

A I-152, 2W-13, parked on the ramp at El Prat air base near Barcelona during 1941. Later this aircraft had its code changed from 2W to C-9. The aircraft was used as a trainer with the *Ejercito del Aire* and had the OP-1 gunsight deleted. (Juan Arraez Cerda)

craft each. Sixty-two were held up in transit by the French government, while the remaining thirty-one I-152s were transported on trucks organized by the French Communist party to Sabadell, where the new fighters were assembled during December of 1938 and January of 1939.

Similar as the I-15 ***Chato*** which was already in Spanish service, the I-152 received the same 'CC' (***Caza Chato/Chato*** fighter) code letters on the fuselage. During its brief Republican service, the new fighter was dubbed semi-officially as the "***Superchato***."

One I-152, flown by Alfredo Dealbert, was destroyed after it crashed into a tank truck. Another fighter crashed when the pilot was unable to pull out of a steep dive in time. The remaining aircraft were formed into three nine-aircraft squadrons, with the remainder being held in reserve. The formation, under the command of Emilio Galera Macias became operation during the final stage of the Spanish Civil War. The I-152 participated in some ground attack missions before being transferred to Vilajuiga for evacuation to France. During its brief operational service, the I-152 suffered no losses in combat operations and had no engagements with enemy fighters.

Before dawn on 5 February 1939, the I-152s crossed the French border and landed without incident at Carcassone airdrome in Southern France. Initially it was planned to evacuate the I-152s to Toulouse-Francazal, but due to bad weather, the formation's leader Emilio Galera Macias decided to head for Carcassone. During the very last moments of the war in Catalonia, numerous packing cases containing unassembled aircraft, some of which were I-152s, were handed over to the Republicans via the French border, but there was no time to assemble them and they were returned to France to prevent their being used by the Nationalists.

In accordance with the Jordana-Berard Agreement, twenty I-152s were returned to Spain. These were given the type code "2W", which was subsequently changed into "C.9" ***(for Caza Tipo 9/***Fighter type 9). These aircraft were allocated to ***Grupo 24 of Regimiento de Caza 23*** at Reus. They served with the ***Ejercito del Aire*** until withdrawn from service in 1954.

Spanish I-152s which were used for training purpose had the armament deleted, the OP-1 gunsight removed and a new flat wind screen installed in place of original windscreen. There were a number of field modifications made to the I-152s when they entered services with the ***Ejercito del Aire***. A trim tab was added to the upper wing aileron, the position light on the wing tip was relocated, with the single position light being replaced by a position light on top and bottom of the upper wing. Not all Spanish I-152s had this modification and there were a

This I-152 was initially serialed VH-5 before being changed into IH-5. The aircraft was finally struck off charge on 11 September 1942. (Keski-Suomen Ilmailumuseo via Hannu Valtonen)

few that had only a single position light on top of the upper wing. Most training I-152s had the wheel pants removed and some also had the propeller spinner deleted.

Finnish I-152s

For many months Soviet Foreign Minister Vyacheslav Molotov had pressed the Finns to cede to the Soviet Union a strip land in southern Finland. The purpose was to project the approaches to Leningrad. Negotiations reached an impasse and on 30 November 1939, Stalin ordered the invasion of Finland.

On 13 March 1940, the Finns could hold out no longer and ceded the Russians the buffer zone they wanted. Losses to the Soviet Air Force during the fighting had been enormous, with some 700 to 900 aircraft being shot down or lost in operational accidents. During the Winter War with Finland between November 1939 and March 1940, a total of five I-152s were captured by the Finns after they made forced landings on Finnish soil. Two out of the five reached ***Lentolaivue 29***, the replenishment and training squadron of the Finnish Air Force. After the cease-fire, the rest of the aircraft were delivered to serve as fighter-trainers. After ***Lentolaivue 29*** was disbanded, its aircraft were handed over to the ***Lentolaivue 34***.

Early in the Continuation War, ***Lentolaivue 34*** was dissolved and the I-152s were assigned as trainers to the ***Taydennyslentolaivue 35*** and two of the aircraft were placed in storage during late 1942. In mid-1943, three aircraft were transferred to the re-established ***Lentolaivue 34*** as target-tows. After the war, the aircraft were placed in storage at the air force depot. The last flight of the I-152 in Finnish Air Force service was on 12 March 1945.

The first two Finnish I-152s initially carried the registration numbers VH-10 and VH-11, while the remaining three biplanes were given serials VH-3 to VH-5. During late 1940, VH-10 and VH-11 were renumbered as VH-1 and VH-2. On 4 June 1942, the confusion regarding the numbering of war booty aircraft was resolved and the aircraft were given the serials IH-1 to IH-5.

A Finnish ground crewman moves a Hucks starter into position to start the engine of this Finish Air Force I-152, VH-2. Before it was captured by the Finns, the aircraft was Yellow 173 of the Soviet Air Force. This particular Polikarpov crashed twice, but was always repaired. On 20 February 1945, the aircraft was placed in storage after 114 hours 50 minutes flying time with the Finnish Air Force. (Keski-Suomen Ilmailumuseo via Hannu Valtonen)

This Finnish Air Force I-152 was undergoing maintenance work and has the forward access panels removed. The aircraft crashed three times while in Finnish service but was returned to flying condition each time. With more as 144 flight hours, this I-152, VH-4, logged more operational time than any other I-152 in Finnish service. (Keski-Suomen Ilmailumuseo via Hannu Valtonen)

When this Finnish Air Force I-152 was captured it was given the serial VH-11 and stationed at Vesivehmaa during the Spring of 1940. (Keski-Suomen Ilmailumuseo via Hannu Valtonen)

Experimental I-152s

I-152TK

A single I-152TK, was built in late 1939, in an attempt to improve the service ceiling of the original I-152 design. It was equipped with two TK-3 turbo-superchargers, but due to their increased weight (308 pounds, 140 kg), the flying characteristics of the aircraft suffered and the project was abandoned.

There were some minor changes introduced on the I-152TK. The armament was deleted and the gun tubes in the nose faired over. The single air intake on top of the engine cowling was also deleted. The spinner was more conical in shape than on production I-152.

The large exhaust stacks on the fuselage sides deleted, being replaced by TK-3 supercharger mounted on each side of the engine cowling. The lower bomb racks were deleted and the upper wing had a trim tab added to the flaps.

I-152DM

The I-152DM (***Dopolnitelny Motor/***auxiliary motor) was fitted with a pair of DPM-2 ramjets beneath the lower wing. This ramjet, developed by Igor A. Merkulov, had a diameter of fifteen inches (40 cm), a length of 5 feet (1.5 meters) and weighed 42 pounds (19 kg). Flight testing commenced in December of 1939, with P. Loginov at the controls, and continued through June of 1940, comprising a total of fifty-four flights. Operation of the DPM-2s boosted the top speed by 11 to 12 mph (18 to 20 km/h). Whenever, the two DPM-2 ramjet engines were not operating, however, the aircraft's speed was considerably slower and the flight characteristics suffered due to the drag from the ramjets.

The I-152TK had on a TK-3 turbosupercharger mounted on each side of the fuselage. The aircraft was equipped with a much more conical propeller spinner than on production I-152s. Additionally, a small trim tab was installed on the upper wing ailerons. (Ivan Ivanow)

The I-152 DM-2 was equipped with each an DPM-2 ramjet engine mounted under the lower wings near the wing tip. Like earlier experiments with a ramjet equipped I-15, it was found that the jets caused considerable drag when not operating and performance suffered. (G.F. Petrov)

PTB Under Fuselage Fuel Tank

A single ski equipped I-152 was tested with a type PTB auxiliary fuel tank mounted under the fuselage centerline between the main landing gear legs. This modification did not progress further and production I-152 lacked a wet point under the fuselage for a under fuselage tank.

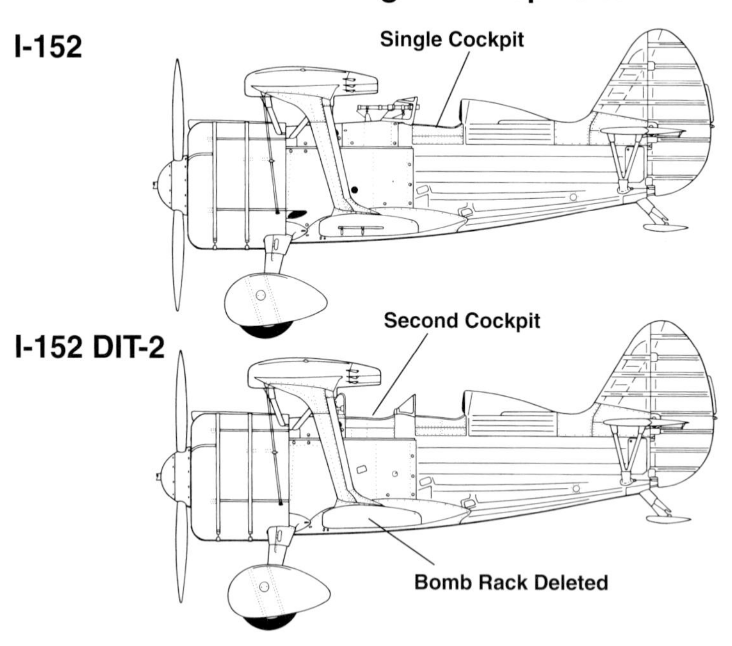

This skid equipped I-152 was modified with an PTB auxiliary fuel tank mounted under the fuselage centerline between the landing gear legs. In the event, this modification did not go into production or service. (G.F. Petrov)

The two seat DIT-2 trainer had the student's cockpit installed in front of the standard cockpit position. The DIT-2 was equipped with a PAK-1 gunsight replacing the standard OP-1 gunsight used on the I-152. (G.F. Petrov)

I-152 DIT-2

During mid-1937, a small series of two seat I-152 DIT-2 (***Dvukhmestny Istrebitel Trenirovochny***/Two seat trainers) were built at GAZ-21. A second cockpit for a student was added in front of the standard cockpit. Fuel capacity was reduced due to the space occupied by the additional cockpit and the aircraft retained the original overall length of the production fighter.

While production I-152s had a M-25V power plant, the DIT-2 was powered by the earlier 715 hp M-25A. Standard I-152s all had adjustable cooling shutters, while the DIT-2 had large, fixed air intakes in the cowling in front of the M-25A power plant.

The performance of the DIT-2 suffered from the increased weight of the second cockpit and reduced power. The maximum ceiling was some 1,968 feet (600 meters) below that of the standard I-152, while the maximum speed was 225 mph (362 km/h).

The armament was reduced to two PV-1 guns and the underwing bomb racks were deleted, but gross weight still increased by 114.5 pounds (52 kg), when compared with the production I-152.

The rear upper wing center section was much more curved on the DIT-2 and there were two small holes in the trailing edge in order to provide the pupil with a better hand hold for boarding the DIT-2 trainer.

The two seat trainer DIT-2 had the student's cockpit in front of the standard cockpit and just under the wing trailing edge. The curved leading edge on the upper wing center section allowed for easier access to the front cockpit. A gunsight was installed in the front windshield and a simple post sight was installed on the starboard side of the rear canopy frame. (Ivan Ivanow)

TsKB-3ter Prototype

During the early stages of the Spanish civil war, pilots flying the I-16 fighter monoplane had encountered difficulty when engaging the extremely nimble Fiat CR.32 biplane fighter in close combat. Pilots of the Italian fighter had employed classic high-G maneuvering dogfight tactics, that put the I-16 at a distinct disadvantage.

Strong factions within the Soviet Air Force had opposed the radical changes in fighter policy heralded by the introduction of the I-16 monoplane and combat reports from Spain led to a vigorous renewal of their demands that development of the fighter biplane be continued.

This question of how future fighter development should proceed was the subject of a special meeting of the Central Committee of the Communist Party, attended by representatives of the Air Force, as well as senior personnel from the aircraft industry. The importance of this meeting was underlined by the fact that Stalin presided over the discussions. The result of this meeting was that the development of biplane fighters would be reinstated.

The main thrust of this continued development was to improve the biplane's aerodynamics to gain higher speeds, while still retaining maneuverability. To reduce drag, the gull upper wing was re-introduced for the next generation biplane fighter. The project was under the leadership of Aleksei Shcherbakov and Aleksei Karyev, two of Polikarpov's principal team leaders. The initial design project received official approval on 11 October 1937.

With little doubt, the experience that the Soviet Union gained during the Spanish campaign was a main factor that led the supreme command of the Soviet Air Force to believe that the biplane fighter was still a modern and efficient weapon, while almost all other countries had accepted the demise of the biplane in favor of monoplane designs.

One of the TsKB-3ter prototypes during the trials held during the Winter of 1938/39. The prototype had trim tab added on each upper wing aileron. The prototype's exhaust system differed from the earlier I-152 in that it had individual exhaust stacks placed around the engine cowling instead of a collector ring. (Ivan Ivanow)

Developement

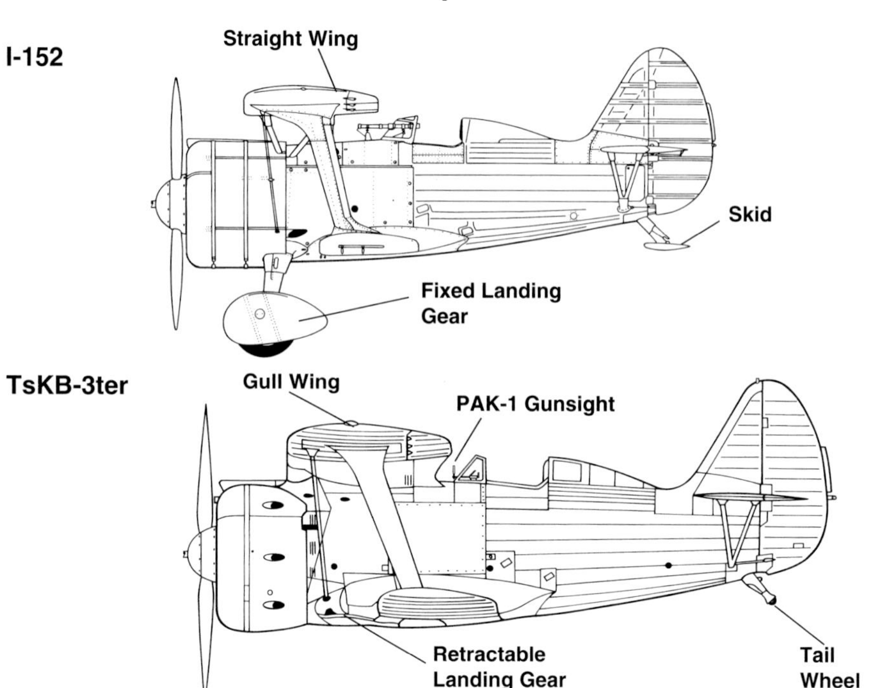

The first prototype of the new biplane, designated the TsKB-3ter, incorporated the Chaika (gull) wing of the earlier I-15, but also included a number of features from the I-152. The basic I-15 fuselage structure was retained, although refined in detail and extensively restressed. The fabric covered wings were of wooden construction, with the upper wing hav-

This TsKB-3ter prototype (Serial 8019) was used for spin tests during the factory trials. The tests were carried out beween 27 June and 4 August of 1940 with test pilot A.I. Zhukov at the controls. (Ivan Ivanow)

The first I-153 prototype was powered by a M-25V power plant. The aircraft was configured with a large propeller spinner and lacked the shuttered cowling front plate. The TsKB-3ter prototypes, pre-production I-153s and early production I-153 were all powered by the M-25V engine adopted from the I-152. (G.F. Petrov)

ing metal-framed fabric covered ailerons with trim tabs. The fuselage was made of KhMA chrome-molybdenum steel alloy tubing with light alloy formers. The forward fuselage was metal covered while the rear fuselage aft of the cockpit was fabric covered. The tail group was made of a fabric covered metal frame, with the rudder being equipped with a trim tab. The prototype also had a stowage compartment built into the dorsal spine behind the cockpit.

The most radical feature of the new fighter was its landing gear. The prototype featured a retractable landing gear with the main landing gear with the gear doors attached rotating ninety degrees and retracting into wells on the underside of the fuselage center section. The gear was retracted by means of a chain drive operated by a handcrank in the cockpit. While the I-15 and I-152 had been equipped with tailskid, the new prototype had a solid, non-retractable tailwheel.

The exhaust configuration of the prototype was similar to the I-15 with five small exhaust stubs, while the number of cowling shutters was reduced and the cooling air intake on cowling lip was also redesigned. The first TsKB-3ter prototype was equipped with an M-25V radial engine driving a V-25 propeller housed in a large conical spinner which was adopted from the I-152. The prototype lacked an engine cover plate, which became standard on the production version.

Two prototypes and the pre-production I-153s were all equipped with a new, Soviet developed, AV-1 variable pitch all-metal propeller and a considerably smaller spinner. While the V-25 propeller could only change pitch on the ground, the AV-1's pitch could be changed hydraulically by a Type R-2 pitch control installed in the cockpit. The AV-1 propeller could be identified by two round balance weights installed on the front of the propeller hub.

Armament of the prototype differed from the earlier I-15 and I-152 in that the PV-1 machine guns were replaced by ShKAS 7.62MM weapons. The ShKAS gun had a rate of fire of 1,800 rounds per minute and had been developed especially for aircraft use. The initial armament installation on the three prototypes caused a number of problems during testing and a young designer named Artyom Mikoyan was assigned to solve the problem. Mikoyan would later gain fame as half of the MiG design team.

The first of three prototypes left assembly line during October of 1938. After completing factory testing they were transferred to the Scientific Test Institute of the Soviet Air Force. During these trials, one of the prototypes crashed, and subsequent investigations showed that the crash was caused by engine overheating which had led to engine failure. This problem was also solved by Mikoyan, who was then assigned to work for the Polikarpov Design Bureau.

While all production I-152s had been equipped with the OP-1 gunsight, the TsKB-3ter and all production I-153s had this sight replaced by the more advanced PAK-1 (***Prizel Aviazionnyj Kollimatornyj***/Aviation Gunsight), which was, in fact, a copy of the French Clair gunsight. After successful testing, the TsKB-3ter was cleared for production under the designation I-153.

This pre-production I-153 was assigned to the test program at Zhukovsky. The retractable landing gear rotated ninety degrees to lay flat in wheel wells in the lower fuselage center section. The aircraft carried no national markings. (A.A. Zirnov)

This TsKB-3ter prototype was fitted with a M-25V power plant and tested at Zhukovsky. The aircraft was not fitted with a shuttered cowling front and the air intake on the cowling lip was different from the one fitted to the production I-153. (G.F. Petrov)

Polikarpov I-153

During the Spring of 1939, the first production examples of the new fighter, now designated the I-153, left the assembly lines of GAZ-156 in Moscow and GAZ-1 at Khodinka, Moscow's central airport.

During testing of the first production I-153s at the Scientific Test Institute of the Soviet Air Force, speeds of 228.6 mph (368 km/h) at sea level and a 623 mph (424 km/h) at 11,482 feet (3,500 m) were recorded. This was some twenty-five to twenty-eight mph (41 to 45 km/h) faster than the earlier I-152 and twelve to eighteen mph (20 to 30 km/h) slower than the I-16 monoplane fighter. The I-153 archived a full 360 degree turn in eleven to twelve seconds, attained an altitude of 16,404 feet (5,000 m) in 6.5 minutes for a rate of climb of 2,523 feet per minute and had a ceiling of 28, 543 feet (8,700 m).

The TsKB-3ter prototypes differed from the early production I-153 in a number of ways. An additional exhaust stub was added to the port lower nose, above the main landing gear wheel well. The three prototypes and a number of pre-production I-153s carried a single bomb rack under each lower wing tip, while production I-153s had two racks under each wing. While the TsKB-3ter prototype had a single vent on the lower fuselage behind the cowling, the production I-153 had two vents. Early production aircraft had a small propeller spinner, while most production versions deleted the spinner.

Most early production aircraft had provision for a RSI-3 radio with the antenna mast being mounted on the inboard panel of the starboard upper wing, along with a small mast mounted on tip of the fin. Often, only the lead I-153 within a formation would be equipped with both transmitter and receiver equipment, while the remaining aircraft would be equipped with only a receiver or had no radio at all.

The first production batches were all equipped with the 775 hp M-25V power plant, while later I-153s were re-engined with the 1,000 hp M-62. The M-62 was a Soviet copy of the Wright-Cyclone R-1820 G-5 engine. While the M-25V had a single-speed supercharger, the M-62 had a two-speed supercharger giving it better altitude performance. Use of the M-62 power plant resulted in an increase in weight of 103 pounds. The dry weight of the M-25V was 1,012 pounds (459 kg) while the M-62 weighed 1,115 pounds (506 kg). Most I-153 all had a front cowling cooling plate, while a few had the plate removed in the field to improve cooling during operation.

Another common field modification was the removal of the landing gear well fairing plate and gear doors, since these were often damaged during operations from rough landing

A Yellow tailed early production I-153, Red 6, of 8th Fighter Regiment, Black Sea Fleet. This unit was based at Kacha airfield near Sevastopol. (Andrew Zinchuck)

A I-153 of the 7th Fighter Aviation Regiment which was based in the Leningrad district. The original Olive Green camouflage was modified with Black on the uppersurfaces. This I-153 carried no tactical number. (Ivan Ivanow)

Development

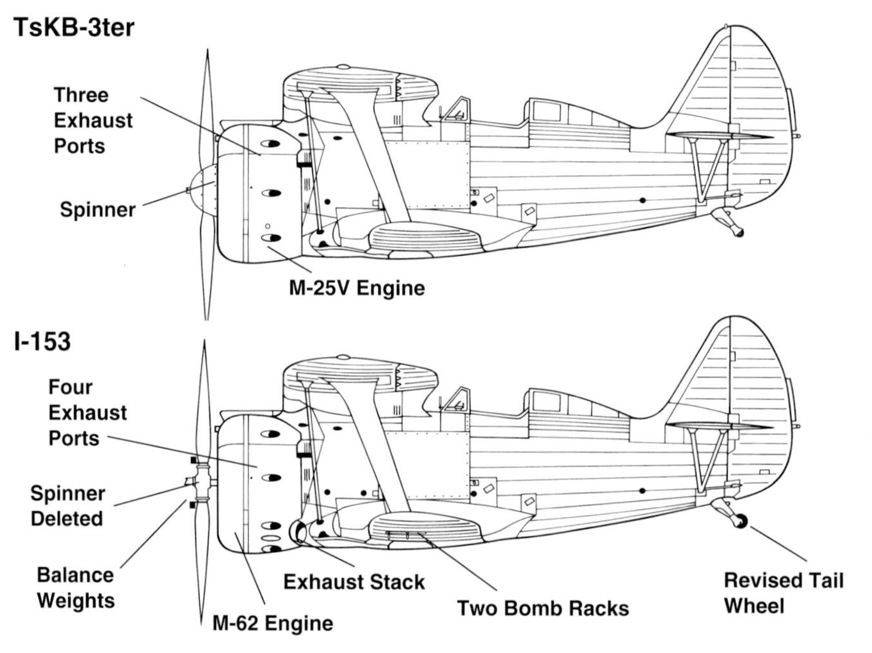

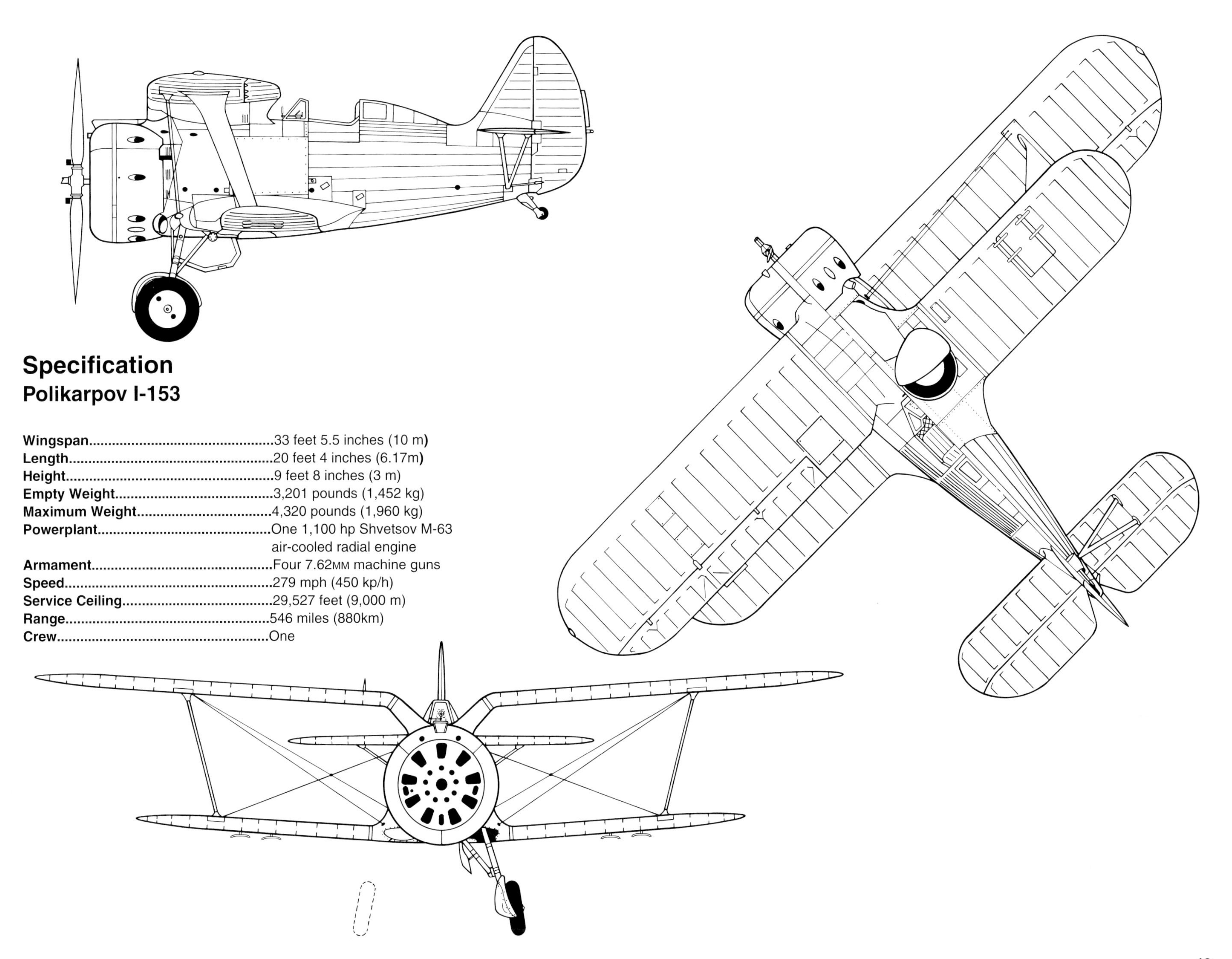

Specification
Polikarpov I-153

Wingspan	33 feet 5.5 inches (10 m)
Length	20 feet 4 inches (6.17m)
Height	9 feet 8 inches (3 m)
Empty Weight	3,201 pounds (1,452 kg)
Maximum Weight	4,320 pounds (1,960 kg)
Powerplant	One 1,100 hp Shvetsov M-63 air-cooled radial engine
Armament	Four 7.62MM machine guns
Speed	279 mph (450 kp/h)
Service Ceiling	29,527 feet (9,000 m)
Range	546 miles (880km)
Crew	One

This I-153, White 93, has four Type RO rocket rails for RS-82 air-to-ground rockets and an additional bomb rack on the lower outer wing panel. The main landing gear doors have been removed, a common practice during rough field operations. (Robert Bock)

grounds. During the Winter, a number of I-153s were equipped with ski landing gear. When skis were fitted, the main landing gear doors were deleted and the wheel well fairing plate was reduced, with the well being covered by a sheet metal plate.

The armament included four ShKAS 7.62MM machine guns with an ammunition supply of 650 rounds per gun. Late production batches had the manual firing mechanism replaced by a pneumatic system. All I-153s had provision for two bomb racks under each lower wing, each having a capacity of 220 pounds (100 kg). These racks could carry either two 110 pound (50

During the early stage of the war, the I-153 saw wide spread combat in the ground support role. These I-153s are all armed with eight RS-82 unguided rockets (four per wing). The I-153 in the foreground has the shuttered front cowling plate removed. (Klaus Niska Collection)

Two I-153s of the 7th Fighter Aviation Regiment, Soviet Baltic Fleet. The aircraft in the background was being started with the aid of a Hucks starter type truck. The aircraft carried a small tactical number, Yellow 2, on the fuselage side behind the cockpit. (Ivan Ivanow)

kg) bombs, four 55 pound (25 kg), eight 22 pound (10 kg) bombs or ChAB-25 and AOCh-15 chemical weapons (either mustard or phosgene gas). Bomb types included the AO-10, AO-20M or the FAB-50M series of bombs.

Beside chemical bombs, the I-153 could also carry a chemical agent dispenser, the VAF-6M (***Vylivnoj Aviazionnyj Pribor***/Chemical Aviation Container) on the underwing racks. The VAP-6M weighed 22 pounds (10.2 kg) and carried a total of 10 gallons (38 liters) of mustard gas or phosphorus. It took three to four seconds to dispense the chemical agents from the tanks over enemy troops. Using the same container as the chemical weapons, a liquid fire dispenser ZAP-6 (***Zashigatelnyj Aviazionnyj Pribor***/Liquid Fire Aviation Container) had also been developed for use on the I-153. A smaller container was added under the main body which contained hydrogen sulfide to ignite the phosphorous when it left the upper container. There were a number of such raids flown with I-153s during the war, dropping burning phosphorous from the ZAP-6 containers on German troops on the Eastern front.

Eight RO rocket rails, for RS-82 unguided rockets, could also be mounted, four per wing, in place of the standard bomb racks. The I-153 could also carry two 21 gallon (80 liter) or 26 gallon (100 liter) fuel tanks in place of the weapons.

Service of the type under front-line combat conditions over Mongolia soon revealed a number of shortcomings with the I-153. Vibration caused the strip covering the wing box to separate, while the lack of a firewall soon became a problem. The ailerons often vibrated and the exhaust stacks frequently disintegrated. Both, the M-25V and the M-62 power plants were generally considered as far from reliable, and the main landing gear often failed or collapsed during a hard landing.

To correct these problems, the I-153 was progressively improved. From early 1940 onward, the M-62 engine was replaced by the 1,100 hp M-63 power plant. Despite its increased

A I-153 undergoing experimental trials with a ski landing gear. This aircraft was unusual in that it carried no underwing bomb racks and the shuttered cowling plate was removed. The entire engine cowling was painted Silver. (Zdenek Hurt)

power, the new engine led to a increase of only 15 pounds (7 kg). During the Second World War, when damaged I-153 were returned to repair depots, the original power plants were often replaced with M-63. Instead of using a Hucks-starter device, the I-153 was equipped with a self starter.

Despite its obsolescence, the I-153 was numerically the second most important fighter in the Soviet Union when Germany invaded the country on 22 June 1941. Red Air Force officials would not let the I-153 production line come to a halt before modern Soviet fighters, such as the MiG-3 and LaGG-3 were available for mass production. This was done to keep the skilled workers and staff at the State Aircraft Factories employed.

During its production life, between the Spring of 1939 and late 1940, a total of 3,437 I-153s were produced at GAZ-1 and GAZ-156. GAZ-1 switched in August of 1940 to the more advanced MiG-3.

The I-153 marked the end of the fighter biplane in the Soviet Air Force. The heyday of the biplane, with its struts and bracing wires, had passed while the Chaika was still on the drawing boards, and even concessions, such as retractable landing gear, could not seriously prolong its life. The I-153 was an anachronism, entering service at a time when the biplane fighter had long since been eclipsed by the monoplane fighter.

Early production versions of the I-153 were delivered with Olive Green uppersurfaces over Light Blue undersurfaces. The Red Star national markings had a thin Black outline and had a small Black circle within the star. The interplane struts was usually painted Light Blue. Some

This I-153, White 93, nosed over during a crash landing in 1943, nearly ripping the engine completely off its mounts and damaging both the upper and lower wing tips. (G.F. Petrov)

A Soviet Air Force pilot boards his I-153, White 45, for another mission. This aircraft carries a camouflage scheme of of Olive Green and Dark Green on the uppersurfaces over Light Blue undersurfaces. In the background is a wooden shelter housing another I-153. No national markings were carried on the wing uppersurfaces. (G.F. Petrov)

This early I-153 warms up for another ground attack mission. This aircraft was modified with underwing rocket rails for two RS-82 rockets on each wing. The fighter had a two tone camouflage of Olive Green and Dark Green on the uppersurfaces. (G.F. Petrov)

Ground crewmen ready this Soviet Navy I-153, White 5, for a mission. The use of the Hucks starter made this type very vulnerable to enemy surprise attacks on their airfields. This aircraft has the lower main landing gear wheel covers, normally attached to the wheels, removed for operations from rough fields. (G.F. Petrov)

I-153s used in Fighter Aviation Regiments during the pre-war period, had no national markings on top of the upper wing, while the national markings on the lower wing were always carried. Tactical numbers were not outlined on overall White or Silver I-153s.

The Winter War with Finland, during the Winter of 1939/1940, revealed that overall Silver was an excellent snow camouflage. As a result of Winter War experience, there were a number of aircraft delivered in an overall Silver lacquer finish. Some I-153s had a Silver fuselage and wings, with only the upper wing uppersurfaces painted in Olive Green. There were also a number Silver aircraft hand painted with Olive Green patches on the aircraft uppersurfaces.

When the war with Germany started in the Summer of 1941, there were a number of I-153s transferred to the ground attack role. A number of these received a two tone uppersurface camouflage of Olive Green and Light Green or Olive Green and Black-Green. In late June of 1941 an order was issued to delete the Black circle from the national markings, and that no national markings would be carried on the wing uppersurfaces.

The tactical numbers applied in wartime varied from unit to unit. Some Fighter Regiments had the tactical number painted on the rudder, some preferred large two or three digit numbers on the fuselage. Sometimes the national markings and the tactical number on the fuselage had a thin White outline.

Combat

At Khalkin-Gol, a river near the border of Outer Mongolia and Manchuria, the Soviets were engaged in a border war with Japan. Due to this incident, Soviet Air Force elements supporting the 1st Army Group received a priority in the supply of the new I-153 fighter.

This nosed over I-153 was inspected by a German soldier. The main landing gear wheels of White 4 are missing and the aircraft still has major damage to the wing near the inboard port bomb rack. The tailwheel was a feature first introduced on the I-153, the earlier I-15 and I-152 had tailskids. (ECPA DAA-1903 L-13)

The full-scale, but undeclared, conflict with Japanese forces along part of the ill-defined Manchurian-Mongolian border, had begun on 11 May 1939 and rapidly escalated. During one major encounter at Khalkin-Gol, the Red Army blocked the Japanese advance in Manchuria and in late August, General Zhukov went on the offensive against the Japanese on the Manchurian-Mongolian border, gaining victory at Khalkin-Gol on 16 September 1939.

Twenty I-153s, fresh off the assembly line were sent by rail across the Soviet Union to the railhead at Cita, where they were collected by the pilots of the 70th Fighter Aviation Regiment, under the command of Major Sergej Gritsevets. The unit flew its first operational sortie with the I-153 on 25 July 1939, engaging in a dogfight with Japanese Type 97 fighters just over the Russo-Mongolian side of the battle field. During the aerial duel, which only lasted five minutes, two Japanese Type 97s were shot down by the Soviet fighters.

During the Winter War with Finland, the Soviet Air Force enjoyed fewer successes. The Soviet effort began with thoughts of a quick victory, but soon the Soviet military found itself stalemated as the Finns displayed fierce resistance. As a result, Stalin had to deploy forty-five rifle divisions and 3,000 aircraft to the front. The most successful airstrike performed by the

When the Wehrmacht captured the Russian forward airbases bombed during earlier Luftwaffe attacks, they found them littered with wrecked I-153s. These aircraft, along with other Soviet Air Force aircraft, were taken to a storage depot on the edge of Minsk aerodrome. (Bundesarchive 265-39-32)

A number of I-153s on the Minsk aerodrome in Belorussia during June of 1941 were stripped by trophy hunters. The national markings were cut off the fuselage of Red 9. The Silver winter camouflage was not applied on the wing upper surfaces. The national marking were carried on the wing uppersurface in the pre-war style. (Bundesarchive)

Soviet Air Force occurred on 29 February 1940, when forty I-153 and I-16 fighters attacked the airfield at Ruokalahti. Three Gloster Gladiators were destroyed on the ground and a further two Gladiators and a Fokker D XXI were shot down in the battle.

When Germany crossed the Soviet border on 22 June 1941, there were 1,549 I-153s allocated to the Western Military Districts and about 50 percent of them were destroyed on the ground. Some units had lower losses than others and in the 11th Mixed Aviation Division, which consisted of the 2nd Fighter Aviation Regiment and the 122nd Fighter Aviation Regiment, there were some fifty-three I-16s and I-153s which survived the disaster.

The German invasion came at the worst possible time for the Soviet Air Force, since new aircraft were not available in large numbers and its pilots were not fully trained on the new generation aircraft. During the Summer of 1941, the backbone of the Soviet Air Force were Polikarpov fighters (I-152, I-153 and I-16s) and the average Soviet pilot lacked the skill, experience and training the Germans had in their more advanced Messerschmitts.

In the Kiev Military District in the Ukraine, there were a total of 1,296 fighters assigned to seventeen Fighter Aviation Regiments. The majority of these, a total of 980, were obsolete Polikarpov I-153s and I-16s. During the early stages of the invasion, the 72nd Combined Regiment of the Northern Fleet, equipped with seventeen I-153s, was the only fighter protection available for the Kola Peninsula. The 8th Fighter Regiment of the Black Sea Fleet operated the I-153 from Kacha airfield in the area of Sevastopol. On the first day of the war, four I-153s attacked a convoy of German trucks and were jumped by eight Messerschmitt Bf-109Es. During the following combat, two of the Messerschmitts were shot down, but such victories were the exception during the Summer of 1941. Usually, the Bf-109 was more than a match for the I-153, but the aircraft could be successful against Luftwaffe bombers. Some I-153s were assigned to night interception units to combat night bombing raids.

With the arrival of more modern fighters, such as the Yak-1, LaGG-3, and MiG-3, the I-153 was relegated to training units or assigned to ground attack duty. The biplane was suited for its new role, and a number of ground attack units equipped with I-153s were still serving well into 1943.

This I-153, Yellow 3, was part of the *Russenparadies* (Russian Paradise) at *Unter den Linden Avenue* in the center of Berlin. The damaged original interplane strut was replaced by two X' shaped, fabric covered tubes by the Germans. On 18 May 1942, the Communist Youth Organization under leadership of Herbert Baum, destroyed most of the equipment, including the I-153. (Vannu Valtonen)

Foreign I-153s

Chinese I-153

The immediate problem of replacing the large numbers of aircraft lost by the Chinese Air Force during 1940, was met by an urgent purchase from the Soviet Union. A total of ninety-three I-153s were supplied to re-equipped the 3rd, 4th and 5th Fighter Groups of the Chinese Air Force. Deliveries began during early 1940 and these aircraft were to be the last supplied to China from the Soviet Union. In April of 1941, shortly before the German invasion, the Soviet Government signed a neutrality pact with Japan, cutting off supplies to the Chinese government.

That time had run out for the biplane fighter was clearly demonstrated during engagements between the I-153s and Japanese Zero. On 14 March 1941, ten Nakajima B5N1s, escorted to Chengtu by twelve Zeros, were intercepted by thirty-one I-153s of the 5th Group and the 28th Squadron. While the I-153s could have easily downed the bombers, they had no chance against the escorting Zeros. The Chinese admitted the loss of sixteen I-153s (eight pilots being killed, including the group commander and his deputy). When it became clear that the I-153 was no challenge for the Zero, most of the remaining I-153s were tasked with interception missions against Japanese bombers and were instructed to avoid combat with the Zero.

China's situation would have seemed quite hopeless except for the prospects of increased American aid. On 1 June 1941, the Chinese Air Force had a total of eighty-nine I-153 and I-16 fighters, as well as about ninety assorted American aircraft, mostly trainers. Before American Lend-Lease started for China, the Polikarpov I-152, I-153 and I-16 remained the backbone of the Chinese Air Force.

Chinese I-153s operated without the shuttered cowling front plate standardized on most Soviet Air Force I-153s. Chinese I-153s carried standard Soviet camouflage of Olive Green uppersurfaces and Light Blue undersurfaces with the Chinese national marking carried on the wing undersurfaces. Only a few I-153s carried the Blue-White striped rudder. Chinese I-153s usually carried a small White serial number on the fin and some carried a four digit White tactical number on the fuselage side behind the cockpit.

A total of ninety-three I-153s were delivered to China. Chinese Air Force I-153s carried no national markings on the wing uppersurfaces or fuselage. The tactical number, 2706, was carried on the fuselage side in White. This fighter was equipped with a pair of underwing drop tanks. (San Diego Aerospace Museum)

This German I-153 (Serial 8245) was later handled over to the Finnish air force, where it became IT-30. All the I-153s which were collected by Finnish pilots on 7 December 1942, carried no registrations or fuselage codes. (Keski-Suomen Ilmailumuseo via Hannu Valtonen)

German I-153s

During the German attack on the Soviet Union, the Luftwaffe captured a number of I-153s on forward airfields in Lithuania, Latvia, Estonia, Ukraine and Belorussia, although German documents reveal that a I-153 was tested by the E2 Department at Rechlin during December of 1940, some six months before the invasion of the Soviet Union.

A small number of captured I-153s were assigned to the short lived ***1. Ostfliegerstaffel*** (1st East Flier Squadron). This was a squadron manned by Soviet volunteers who wanted to fight against the Soviet government under Stalin. They were part of the ***Russkaia Osvoboditelnaia Armiia*** (Russian Liberation Army). The unit; however, soon lost favor and the project of forming a Russian air wing within the Luftwaffe, under the command of ex-Soviet Air Force Colonel V.I. Maltzev, was quietly phased out.

The I-153 was of little interest to the Germans and some of the undamaged I-153s saw limit-

This overall Gray I-153 (Serial 8252) carried the Luftwaffe fuselage registration code H4 + MB. It was later given to the Finnish Air Force and flown from Hildesheim Air Base in Germany to Finland by a Finnish pilot on 27 August 1943. It became IT-31 in Finnish service. (Keski-Suomen Ilmailumuseo via Hannu Valtonen)

ed service as training and liaison aircraft. At least one I-153 (Serial 7068), belonging to the Stab LLG 1 was damaged after it suffered a landing gear failure during landing at Hildesheim Airfield in Central Germany on 30 July 1942.

A I-153 and a MiG-3, captured on the Eastern Front in the Summer of 1941, were dismantled and shipped to ***Beutepark der Luftwaffe 5*** (Sample Collection 5) at Nanterre-La Folie on the Paris - St. Germain railway line in France. The I-153 was in a non-airworthy condition and carried standard Soviet Air Force camouflage and the tactical number, Red 9. When advancing French troops liberated the area during August of 1944, they found to their surprise, a number of British and American aircraft, and the nearly undamaged I-153. After the war, the Soviet fighter was transferred to the Musee de l'Air at Le Bourget airfield.

A number of I-153s were also used in displays of war booty (captured) material within the Third Reich. A White camouflaged I-153, Yellow 3, was taken to Berlin as part of a public exhibition of Soviet military equipment, called the ***Russenparadies*** (Russian Paradise). Since the original interplane struts had been damaged, they were replaced by fabric covered 'X' shaped tubes. On 18 May 1942, the Communist Youth Organization under the leadership of Herbert Baum, destroyed the I-153 and other items of Soviet equipment by burning the exhibit.

Nine undamaged I-153s were delivered from Vienna, Austria to the Finnish Air Force on 7 December 1942, and another aircraft was delivered on 27 August 1943 from Hildesheim.

Finnish I-153s

During the Winter war with Finland (November of 1939 through March of 1940), eight I-153 aircraft were captured after they forced landed in Finland. The first I-153 was given the registration VH-101, while the others received the numbers VH-12 to VH-18.

This Finish Air Force I-153 was delivered to Finland carrying the German registration code H4+MB. The I-153 was reserialed IT-31 and was placed in storage at Utti Air Base in December of 1943. The aircraft carries a Yellow fuselage identification band. (Keski-Suomen Ilmailumuseo via Hannu Valtonen)

A Finnish I-153 (VH-12) at Turku on 13 June 1941, shortly before the start of the Continuation War. During the short period of peace between the wars, the I-153s carried no Yellow fuselage identification band. (Keski-Suomen Ilmailumuseo via Hannu Valtonen)

On 25 June 1941, the Soviet Air Force bombed Turku in three waves of forty aircraft, starting the Continuation War. During the early stage of the conflict, three additional I-153s were captured, receiving the registrations VH-19 to VH-21. During 1942, the prefix was changed from VH to IT.

An additional nine I-153s were purchased from Germany on 18 November 1942. These aircraft, all painted overall Light Gray, were handed over to the Finnish Air Force at Vienna, Austria on 7 December 1942 . During the ferry flight to Finland, three were damaged and arrived later. Another aircraft was handed over on 27 August 1943. These new I-153s were numbered IT-22 to IT-31. A total of twenty-one I-153s were taken into the inventory of the Finnish air arm.

In Finnish service the I-153 was re-armed, having four of 7.70MM Browning M.39 machine guns, in place of the original Soviet ShKAS 7.62MM guns. In addition, a BBC.AAK-1 gunsight replaced the original Soviet PAK-1 gunsight.

The I-153s were assigned to the Naval Headquarters for patrol, anti-submarine operations, and attacking Soviet ground troops. Finnish I-153s had several engagements with Soviet aircraft during the war. On 11 November 1942, Pilot Officer O. Puro shot down a Pe-2 bomber near Peninsaari. On 24 March 1943, a Finnish I-153 patrol was engaged by two Soviet Chaikas. One of the Finnish fighters was damaged and had to make a forced landing on the ice on the Soviet side near Penisaari. Pilot Officer Puro landed on the ice and picked up the other pilot, flying him back to base clinging to the wing of his aircraft. The other I-153s in the patrol destroyed the damaged I-153 to prevent it from falling into Soviet hands. A group of four Finnish I-153s made the last combat flight of the Chaika during the war. They were intercepted by Soviet Lend-Lease Bell P-39s, although there were no losses to either side during the engagement. On 24 February 1945, all remaining Finnish I-153 were retired.

Experimental I-153s

I-153V

A single I-153V (***Vysotnyi***/High altitude) was built during late 1939, equipped with two TK-3 turbosuperchargers mounted on both sides of the M-63 power plant. The I-153V had all armament deleted and the gun openings in the nose faired over, although the PAK-1 gunsight was retained. A semicircle heat resistant piece of metal was added to the fuselage sides, just behind the exhaust stubs.

During testing at Zhukovsky Experimental Base, the I-153V reached a speed of 275 mph (443 km/h) at 19,685 feet (6,000 meters) but, in all other respects, its performance was inferior to the standard I-153.

I-153 DM-2

The I-153 DM-2 (***Dopolnitelny Motor***/auxiliary motor) was fitted with a pair of DPM-2 ramjets mounted under the lower wings as an engine test bed, similar to those mounted on an earlier I-152. Tests flown from the Zhukovsky Test and Experimental base revealed that the DPM-2s boosted overall speed by eleven to twelve mph (18 to 20 km/h), but when not operating, their drag cut speed considerably. Additionally, the aircraft's flying characteristics were remarkable inferior due to the drag of the two ramjets.

The testbed, an overall Silver I-153, had been heavily modified in the nose section. The armament was deleted, however, the PAK-1 gunsight was retained. The air intake on top of the engine cowling was deleted and two new air intakes were fitted in the leading edge of the gull wing. Additionally, the two fuselage vents, standard on all production I-153s, were also deleted. This experimental I-153 was later modified with a pair of more powerful DPM-4 ramjets under the designation I-153 DM-4. On 3 October 1940, the DPM-4 equipped testbed attained a speed of 267 mph (430 km/h) at an altitude of 6,561 feet (2,000 meters) followed by another flight on 27 October, during which a speed of 273 mph (440 km/h) was reached.

The I-153 DM-4 was equipped with two DPM-4 ramjets which ran on gasoline with an ethyl-alcohol additive. The testbed did not carry any armament and the cooling air intake on top of the engine cowling was replaced by two air inlets on top of the fuselage center section. (Ivan Ivanow)

The I-153GK was equipped with a pressure cabin developed by Aleksei Shcherbakov. The entire cockpit capsule weighed some 99 pounds (45 kg). The rear sliding canopy folded back into the head rest area and the normally fabric covered dorsal spine was replaced by a glazed section. (Ivan Ivanow)

I-153GK

The I-153GK (***Germeticheskyi Kabina***/Pressurised Cabin) was a high altitude experimental fighter, equipped with a pressurized cockpit developed by Aleksei Shcherbakov. The overall Silver I-153 retained its full standard armament. When open, the canopy was housed within the head rest fairing. A 6MM Plexiglas panel was mounted to cover the instrument panel, which formed a part of the pressure cabin frame. The normally fabric covered dorsal spine was replaced by a clear Plexiglas fairing, which gave the pilot excellent rearward view. On port side, below the cockpit, a square access hatch was introduced, which was not a standard feature on production I-153s.

I-153 BS-M-62

Combat experience revealed that to destroy an enemy aircraft it was not always best to have a high rate of fire, sometimes a larger caliber armament was needed. As a result, the Polikarpov Design Bureau developed two variants of the I-153 armed with large caliber weapons.

The I-153 BS-M-62 had its four ShVAK 7.62MM guns replaced by four 12.7MM Berezin BS (***Berezina Skorostrelny***/Berezin Fast Firing Gun) machine guns, with a rate of fire of 800 rounds per minute. The I-153 BS-M-62 was produced in substantial numbers.

I-153 P-M-62

The I-153 P-M-62 (P=***Pushechnyi***/Cannon armed) had two synchronized 20MM ShVAK (***Shpitalny-Vladimirova Aviatsionnaya Krupnokalibernaya***/Shpitalny-Vladimirov Large Caliber Cannon) cannons in place of its standard weapons. The ShVAK had a rate of fire of 750 to 800 rounds per minute. The I-153 P-M-62 was also built in substantial numbers.